K★19

THE WIDOWMAKER

THE SECRET STORY OF THE SOVIET NUCLEAR SUBMARINE

PETER HUCHTHAUSEN
CAPT., USN (RET.)

NATIONAL GEOGRAPHIC

WASHINGTON, D.C.

PUBLISHED BY THE NATIONAL GEOGRAPHIC SOCIETY
1145 17th Street N.W., Washington, D.C. 20036

First printing 2002
COPYRIGHT © 2002 NATIONAL GEOGRAPHIC SOCIETY

Printed in the U.S.A.

CHAPTER OPENER PHOTO CREDITS

Page 1: The *K-19*, 1972. Courtesy of the Royal Air Force. *Page 9:* Nikolai Voronkov,
engineer aboard the *Novorossysk*. Courtesy of Nikolai P. Muru. *Page 25:* Nuclear submarine hull
section, Severodvinsk. Courtesy of Joshua Handler. *Page 49:* Captain Nikolai Zateyev. Courtesy
of Antonina Zateyev. *Page 61:* Nuclear submarine building hall, Severodvinsk. Courtesy of the
Bellona Foundation. *Page 79:* Hotel-class subs at the pier in Polyarny. Courtesy of Peter
Huchthausen. *Page 111:* Chief engineer Captain Third Rank Anatoly Kozyrev, aboard the
K-19. Courtesy of the Historical Museum of the Northern Fleet, Murmansk. *Page 149:* Plaque
commemorating the victims of the 1961 *K-19* accident, Cathedral of Saint Christopher the
Mariner, St. Petersburg. Courtesy of Peter Huchthausen. *Page 163:* Wreck of the *Novorossysk*,
1956. Courtesy of Nikolai P. Muru. *Page 171:* The *K-19* in Arctic ice. Courtesy of the
Historical Museum of the Northern Fleet, Murmansk. *Page 179:* The *Komsomolets*. Courtesy
of the Bellona Foundation. *Page 189:* Last May Day celebration in Red Square, 1990.
Courtesy of Kathleen Huchthausen. *Page 201:* Nikolai Zateyev. Courtesy of Antonina Zateyev.

CONTENTS

JULY 4, 1961, ABOARD THE *K-19*

PROLOGUE

THE MEN WORKING IN *Compartment Six reported that fire had broken out, with flames of a light blue to violet color appearing over the reactor lid. On orders from the central command post, Compartment Six was sealed. Fires broke out twice, and they were extinguished with equipment that had been readied for this purpose in advance. But why a violet flame? I wondered. Finally, the welding was finished, and the booster pump was activated, connected to a 30-ton tank of fresh water. I went below and made my way to Compartment Six. Standing at the bulkhead were Kozyrev and Vakhromeyev, who reported the situation. As they did so, the bulkhead door opened and Korchilov emerged from the compartment. He ripped off his gas mask and immediately began vomiting a white and yellow foam. He was taken to Compartment One, where a medical post had been set up. All the men who had been in Compartment Six were exposed to massive amounts of radiation, the doses they sustained going far beyond permissible levels.*

We had to try to drain the reactor compartment lower-level sump. The main stripping pump for Compartment Eight had failed; it was out of order. We decided to drain the sump with the main drainage pump for the central post. As soon as we started pumping, the radiation count rose in Compartments Five, Four, and Three. Evidently particulate fission products were being flushed out of the sump and channeled through these other compartments by the main drain pump.

I felt my gorge rise. I went off to my cabin and lay down on my berth. Thoughts of all kinds were racing through my head. I knew I had to take action. The problem now was how to save the crew and the ship. My main worry was the men. Everyone who'd been in Compartment Six was doomed; that much I knew already. But what could I do now? We were still about 1,500 miles from home. If we maintained a speed of ten knots, we'd arrive in six or seven days. We'd all be exposed to ten roentgens per hour at the very least for that entire period. None of us would survive.

— from the memoir of Capt. Nikolai Zateyev

★ ★ ★

ON AUGUST 12, 2000, almost 40 years after the unreported nuclear accident aboard the Soviet submarine *K-19*, the Russian super-submarine *Kursk* exploded and sank in 350 feet of water in the Barents Sea, less than 200 miles from the northern city of Murmansk, taking 118 Russian sailors and engineers to their deaths. The *Kursk* represented the pride of the Russian Navy, greatly reduced in size yet still maintaining an effective submarine force. The *Kursk,* capable of firing cruise missiles and diving to 1,500 feet, was one of a class of 11 submarines that were built to counter Western aircraft carrier battle formations.

Forty-nine top submarine officers, 36 more than the normal complement, were aboard the *Kursk* that day. They had come to observe a test firing of a remarkable new undersea weapon called the *Shkval* torpedo-missile. A super-cavitating missile capable of underwater speeds of more than 200 miles per hour, it was designed as a surface ship and submarine killer. The *Kursk* was testing an improved version of the *Shkval* that had a longer range and used liquid fuel, replacing the earlier solid-fuel system. After a long history of accidents caused by unstable liquid-missile fuel, the Soviet Navy had finally shifted to solid-fuel propellants in the late 1980s. This return to liquid fuel in the new torpedo was intended to save costs in a financially strapped navy. To fire the torpedo-missile out of the launch tube, the new system used monopropellant containing a nitrate-ester-based energy source, which is highly unstable. Similar liquid fuel had caused disastrous explosions in two British diesel submarines in the early post-World War II years.

During the test aboard the *Kursk*, unstable liquid fuel leaked from an older model torpedo and reacted with metals inside the casing, exploding and starting a raging fire in the torpedo room, the first compartment in the bow of the ship. A second massive explosion, with a force equivalent to more than 55 tons of TNT, followed just over two minutes later. The second blast tore open the bow and caused a fire that incinerated most of the submarine forward of the nuclear reactors. Russian submariners who had been involved in earlier tests of the same weapon would later claim that when firing the new weapon the overpressure inside the torpedo room had been so severe and painful that, to lessen the effect, they often opened the watertight hatches between three or four compartments leading astern. If this was what happened aboard the *Kursk*, the subsequent blast destroyed all life aboard as far aft as there were open hatches.

Early attempts to rescue survivors were unsuccessful. After seven days of fruitless rescue efforts, Mikhail Mostok, Chief of Staff of the Northern Fleet, said that he feared the worst. After recovering 12 bodies from the after escape compartment, two months after the accident Russian experts determined, from notes found with the remains of one officer, that 23 crew members had survived the initial blast and had fought their way back to the stern compartment. They died fours hours later when trying to activate an oxygen supply system that exploded when exposed to oily water in the bilges, killing the remaining survivors.

In late September 2001, the hull of the submarine was raised from the ocean floor. The severed forward compartment remained on the bottom. "The tragedy of the *Kursk* is a parable of modern Russia," John Barry observed in *Newsweek*, "a country still grappling with sudden collapse from superpower status, and also with responsibilities of a more open society."

A large lifting device moved the battered hull to a floating drydock near Murmansk. The dock was then pumped dry, exposing the burned and twisted hulk. The hull was carefully searched for the remainder of the missing crew and clues to the cause of the accident. Fifty-six additional bodies were recovered (more later), and the results of the investigation showed that an older model torpedo's liquid fuel had caused the accident. Immediately following an inquiry, Russian President Vladimir Putin removed 18 senior officers within the Northern Fleet, including the commander in chief and most of his senior submarine force commanders. Some of these face criminal charges of dereliction of duty and operating the fleet in an unsafe manner.

★ ★ ★

THE *KURSK* ACCIDENT IS by no means unique in the history of the Russian Navy. The extreme pressure to compete with Western navies for superiority throughout the Cold War drove the Soviet Union to accelerate the production of new ships and weapons platforms at a headlong pace. The Soviet military responded to the pressure for naval superiority by producing submarines quickly, often with disregard for safety protocols, and they hurried these submarines to sea with minimal testing and insufficient crew training. Although their design techniques were competitive with NATO's, the Soviet military leadership proved too inflexible to ensure adequate quality control during mass production of naval vessels. Design and construction flaws were addressed far too slowly. The production and management system also failed to ensure that the ships were safe, and failed to effectively evaluate and implement feedback from the navy crews that tested these sophisticated ships and submarines at sea. The safety and construction shortcomings were responsible for the frequent accidents and heavy loss of life that accompanied the growth of the Soviet Navy from the early post-World War II years to the end of the Cold War.

The catastrophic loss of the *Kursk* came at a time of growing economic hardship for the once formidable, but now withering, armed forces of the Russian Federation, just nine years after the dissolution of the Soviet Union. The *Kursk* may be only the latest in a long series of naval accidents, but it is no longer possible to suppress information about these accidents, since information now flows relatively unfettered from the former closed society of Russia.

The dawning of *glasnost* under Soviet leader Mikhail Gorbachev led to the emergence of the valuable memoirs and transcripts used in this book. I have used accounts by officers and crewmen of ships and submarines who witnessed explosions, sinkings, and many other near disasters. They were eager to relate stories of malfeasance and ineptitude long hidden from public view by a repressive regime. The views in the following pages reflect, for the first time in contemporary naval history, the candid opinions of submarine designers and builders who served in top leadership positions during the twilight years of the Soviet Union as well as noted senior Russian nuclear submariners, including the last commander in chief of the Soviet Navy, Admiral Vladimir N. Chernavin; his first deputy Ivan M. Kapitanets; the chief of navy staff, Konstantin V. Makarov; and two first deputy chiefs of staff for operations, the late Admirals Petr Navoytsev and Ivan Komarov. The conclusions expressed in the book regarding safety and fleet preparedness reflect the views of those senior admirals and more than a dozen Russian atomic submarine commanders, most of whom were involved in serious engineering accidents, or in collisions with U.S. submarines. Many of these unique views were expressed to me while I was serving as the senior U.S. Naval attaché in Moscow 1987-1990 or during research visits to Russia during the period 1991-1996. The personal accounts of accidents focus, whenever possible, on the widespread flaws permeating the fleet, yet demonstrate how Russian navymen fought bravely to keep their ships and submarines from burning and sinking.

Foremost among them is Captain First Rank Nikolai Zateyev, the naval officer who commanded the *K-19*, the first Soviet nuclear-powered submarine equipped with ballistic missiles. His harrowing encounter with lethal nuclear radiation is one of the most frightening accidents in the annals of the sea. Captain Zateyev's personal memoir, translated here, offers an unparalleled firsthand look at the early period of Soviet nuclear submarines and echoes the views expressed by most Russian submarine commanders concerning the conditions within the fleet and the hardships they faced keeping their submarines ready for sea.

The uncovering of previously censored material also sheds light on the circumstances of these accidents. As a navy veteran who closely followed Soviet Navy developments for more than 30 years, I was particularly struck by the heroism exhibited by Soviet naval officers and crewmen in the thick of catastrophic events. For that reason, the book tries to portray as vividly as possible these tests of courage and despair. The memoir also points out the underlying causes of many of the unfortunate accidents that plagued the Soviet Navy throughout the Cold War.

The following account begins with a look at the early post-World War II years of frantic attempts to replace shipbuilding facilities devastated by the Nazi invasion and explains Marshal Joseph Stalin's grandiose plans for a world-class navy. It provides details of selected early submarine accidents and the largest peacetime naval disaster in history, which were caused by shoddy safety practices, weaknesses of navy officer training, and political cronyism, widespread in the fleet following the years of wartime instability. The book shows how the American progress in post-war submarine development and nuclear power drove the Soviet atomic power program to speed its expansion of a fleet of barely seaworthy, missile-carrying submarines. Submarine construction and crew training methods during the early nuclear power era are compared to show differences in emphasis by the United States and the Soviet navies. The behavior of Soviet shipbuilding authorities and the navy leadership in the scramble to keep abreast of Western naval developments are also described. Finally the book turns to the threat that still lurks in the waters surrounding the former Soviet Union posed by discarded reactors and nuclear waste and the enormity of the task of cleaning the environmental residue that faces Russia today.

The Soviet Union was long known for burying its secrets. In the Cold War years (1948 to 1991), the horrific casualties sustained by the Soviet Navy were hidden from the Russian people. Nuclear waste was dumped into the world's oceans. The grim results have now been uncovered, a legacy that threatens to haunt us for generations.

CHAPTER ONE

 **T**HE SOVIET NAVY'S RED banners, initially hoisted during the Revolution of 1917, were unfurled in 1945 with new zeal following the defeat of Nazi Germany. Out of the devastation of the war Joseph Stalin launched a modern navy designed to catapult his victorious military into a new era as one of the world's largest naval powers. The Soviet Navy charged headlong into the future astride Stalin's ambitious plan to build a modern fleet of cruisers, including the new 20,000-ton *Sverdlov* and 44,000-ton *Stalingrad* classes, as well as aircraft carriers.

Stalin's plans were conceived as the dictator's personal reaction to photos depicting the vast allied fleets arrayed in the Atlantic during the Normandy invasion and in the Pacific, when large combined task forces covered the seas in anchorages as far as the eye could see. Stalin envied the naval strength of Britain and the United States and felt his own weak navy constrained his plans for exporting communism worldwide. In 1948 he would complain that he could not adequately assist the Greek communists in their uprising because "we have no navy."

Stalin was convinced that the Soviet Union needed a navy commensurate with its newfound status as a superpower. The dictator also believed an aggressive naval building program would revitalize Soviet heavy industry, ravaged in the war against Germany. The Soviet Union would build a new navy to provide the supplies to Soviet-sponsored wars of national liberation worldwide. Fast cruisers and submarines would help project Soviet assistance. The navy would become an instrument of global strategy, a "fleet in being," in naval strategist Alfred Thayer Mahan's words. It would be a navy to persuade friends and foes alike of Soviet global power.

To enhance Stalin's idea of a grand navy, the Communist Party of the Soviet Union promoted the rich naval lore of the Russian past, expanding on the popular dreams of the 17th-century Russian tsar Peter the Great and his quest for a large fleet based in warm-water ports. The progressive tsar had made major strides to incorporate shipbuilding techniques from abroad into his dream fleet of powerful warships. He gathered Dutch, English, and German ship designers and naval officers to his cities to plant the seeds of a powerful navy.

Russian history was replete with naval drama and famous sea battles against the Turks, Swedes, and Japanese by naval heroes such as Admirals Fyodor Ushakov, who stormed the island of Corfu in 1799; Pavel Nakhimov, hero of the siege of Sevastopol in 1855; and Stepan Makarov, commander of the Russian Pacific Squadron, who died aboard flagship *Petropavlosk,* sunk in the Russo-Japanese War in 1905. Russia's only naval victories occurred in 1714 against the Swedes in the Baltic Sea and in

1790 against the Turks in the Black Sea. Most of the celebrated Russian naval events were decisive losses, such as the 1904 sinking of the cruiser *Varyag* or the mutiny aboard armored cruiser *Potemkin* in 1917. Not surprisingly, the communist-era propaganda overlooked less glorious events in Russian naval history, like the 1905 Battle of Tsushima, in which the entire Russian fleet was lost to the upstart Japanese navy, and the bloody uprising by Kronstadt sailors in 1921, an early attempt at anti-Bolshevik counterrevolution.

In the immediate post-war years, while the Western Allies rapidly dismantled the largest naval armadas the world had ever seen, Stalin began a systematic rebuilding program. This updated and expanded navy would have a brand-new mission: to project offensive naval power and run offensive naval operations on the high seas. This shift in naval policy, undertaken by a Soviet regime bound to military secrecy and to strict internal security controls, initially drew little attention from the victorious Western Allies. The Western powers were then focusing primarily on developing nuclear weapons and short- and long-range missiles and air forces to deliver them.

A large percentage of Soviet shipyards, ports, inland waterways, and naval infrastructures, including training and maintenance facilities, lay in ruins. The Soviet Union was forced to rebuild these facilities from scratch, and a rapidly expanding core of modern, well-equipped shipyards that incorporated the matériel and machinery newly acquired as the spoils of war emerged. These modern shipyards would soon begin to launch modern surface ships and submarines from their new building ways. Yet until these shipyards produced at capacity, the Soviet Navy was forced to rely on massive amounts of Allied hardware received during the war.

The Soviet Union had accepted several hundred American and British warships along with vast quantities of naval weapons and equipment, including antiaircraft and antisubmarine weapons, marine supplies, machinery, vehicles, and clothing. The Soviets also put to good use war reparations and knowledge acquired from the defeated enemy. The 1945 Berlin Conference, convened to coordinate the partition and dismantling of the remains of the German war machine, awarded the Soviet Union a number of ships from former Axis navies. These ships helped to compensate for wartime losses and helped the Soviets bridge the transition period before their new modern shipyards started to produce in quantity. From the Germans they received the damaged 22,000-ton aircraft carrier *Graf Zeppelin*, the 13,000-ton battleship *Schleswig-Holstein*, the 6,000-ton light cruiser *Nurnberg*, ten destroyers, and ten still-functioning U-boats. From the Italians they received the 24,000-ton battleship *Giulio Cesare*, the light cruiser *Emanuele Filberto Duca d'Aosta*, four destroyers, 14 torpedo boats, and two submarines. From the Japanese they acquired six destroyers and numerous small boats and submarines.

The conquering Soviet forces also acquired vast quantities of naval matériel from the Soviet zone in northern Germany. They commandeered unfinished ships, submarine sections, submarine machinery, factories, and large quantities of scientific and technical data. Included were some intact and some partially completed German U-boats of the exotic XXI, XXIII, and XXVI classes. They also acquired a new hydrogen-peroxide submarine-propulsion technology. These state-of-the-art German submarines and the new propulsion technology were a boon to Soviet naval designers. So too were Japanese submarines of the *I-200* class that fell into Soviet hands during the initial jockeying for the spoils of a defeated Japan. These top-of-the-line Japanese submarines provided Soviet submarine builders with important technology heretofore unknown to them. Yet prime prizes for the future Soviet Navy were the elite German naval construction and weapons specialists seized and spirited east to be exploited in Soviet research and marine design bureaus. The Soviets immediately recognized the value of all these industrial assets. To help exploit them, they set up a large headquarters in occupied Berlin whose task was specifically to sort through vast amounts of technology confiscated from the naval yards.

Entire shipyards and ship construction halls in north German ports were dismantled by the Russians; loaded onto railways, ships, and barges; and transported to the Soviet Union. The loss at sea of the unfinished and damaged German aircraft carrier *Graf Zeppelin* was symptomatic of the massive stripping effort and great haste by the post-war Soviet government. In 1946 the 20,000-ton aircraft carrier was loaded with German shipyard machinery and towed toward Soviet ports. The carrier capsized and sank in the Baltic Sea, the result of poor loading and heavy weather. German naval shipbuilding methods, based on the World War II machinery, technology, and engineering methods, are still used in Russia today. Soviet submarine construction techniques, specifically their individual hull segment assembly, are adaptations of earlier German methods. This technique involves the separate construction of complete submarine sections that are later joined together in covered building halls.

The Soviet Union's post-war territorial gains were equally important in building a world-class navy. Annexing territory after the War, the Russians acquired the year-round blue-water ports they had sought for 300 years. No longer would Russian Navy warships have to be icebound for five months a year. In

1945 the Soviet Union occupied the Baltic states of Lithuania, Estonia, and Latvia as well as most of East Prussia. In addition, after a short time the Soviets gained full use of Baltic ports in Poland and East Germany. The Baltic coastline controlled by the Soviet Navy mushroomed from 75 pre-war miles to one thousand miles, turning the Baltic Sea into a virtual Soviet lake. Soviet territorial gains in the Pacific were also extensive. Following the Japanese surrender in 1945, the U.S.S.R. acquired the Kurile Islands, southern Sakhalin Island, and the northern half of Korea. The Soviet Navy also gained the use of satellite ports on the Black Sea in Bulgaria and Romania. Despite these territorial gains and new access to year-round seaports, the movements of three of the four Soviet fleets—the Pacific, the Baltic, and the Black—remained restricted by Western control of accesses to major sea channels. The Tsugaru, Tsushima, and Soya Straits guarded the Sea of Japan. The Danish controlled the Baltic Sea approaches. And the Black Sea could be accessed only through the Turkish straits. Nevertheless, the new Soviet fleet would soon unfurl its red banners on seas all over the world.

In the six years following World War II, the Soviets placed heavy emphasis on scientific and technological progress despite the heavy cost this imposed on an already devastated population. By 1951 the U.S.S.R. had rebuilt much of its industrial base and was well on its way to achieving its goal of superiority in military and naval hardware. In those six years the Soviet Union built more warships than all other nations of the world combined. Between 1948 and 1950 alone, they produced 50 to 60 submarines a year as they frantically pursued their goal of a submarine force of 500 by 1959. By the mid-fifties the Soviet Navy operated more submarines than Nazi Germany had during the height of the Atlantic U-boat campaign against the

Allies. The Soviet fleets, although still in the early phases of what would become a frenzied build-up, enjoyed a new political and military status in the U.S.S.R.

The Soviet Union's massive naval push was short-lived, though, and faltered when Joseph Stalin died in 1953. A three-year period of struggle ensued among his potential successors, and resulted in the rise of a new Party general secretary, Nikita S. Khrushchev. During the early Khrushchev period the navy commander in chief, Admiral Nikolai G. Kuznetsov, prepared the foundation for a modern fleet powered by atomic energy and capable of depoloying nuclear weapons. The popular Kuznetsov had first become the commander in chief following the decimation of senior navy officer ranks in Stalin's purges of the 1930s, which included Kuznetsov's predecessor, Vladimir Orlov, as well as an estimated 30 percent of the officer corps of the entire armed forces, among them four of the five geographical fleet commanders. Only the Pacific Fleet commander survived, presumably because he was the farthest removed from Moscow. Admiral Kuznetsov, the senior Soviet admiral throughout World War II, briefly served as commander of the Pacific Fleet following the war, then returned to Moscow in 1951 as the Minister of the Navy. In 1953 he became deputy minister of defense and again navy commander in chief.

In 1955 a tragedy ended Kuznetsov's term as commander and ushered in the new regime of Admiral Sergei Gorshkov. The *Novorossysk*, a 24,000-ton battleship, flagship of the Black Sea Fleet, exploded, capsized, and sank in the Soviet's primary Black Sea port of Sevastopol with the loss of 608 seamen. This single event would have far-reaching consequences. The battleship, originally an Italian ship named *Giulio Cesare*, was transferred to the Soviet Navy in February 1949 in accordance with the terms of the Tehran Conference of December 1943, which dismantled the wartime Italian Navy. Revealed for the first time to the Soviet public and the world 33 years after the event, the sinking of the *Novorossysk* was the 20th century's largest peacetime naval disaster.

★ ★ ★

SHORTLY AFTER RETURNING from sea on October 29, 1955, the battleship exploded in Sevastopol harbor. A thousand men were able to leap to safety from the decks and superstructure, but two hours and forty-five minutes after the blast, the massive battleship rolled over and settled into the three-meter-thick mud while her own crew and rescue parties from nearby ships were still desperately trying to save her. She settled bow down in 50 feet of water with hundreds of crewmen entombed inside the hull. Many of those trapped were able to stay alive for some time on the air remaining in the overturned compartments. Yet despite frantic tapping from inside the hull, still heard 36 hours after capsizing, rescuers retrieved only nine survivors from her bilges by cutting through the thick armored skin of the ship.

While the crew were pulling burned and injured shipmates from the oil-soaked harbor, one engineer-seaman, named Nikolai Voronkov, was fighting for his life deep in the bowels of the battleship. Immediately after the explosion Nikolai raced to his battle station, located in a diesel generator space four levels below the main deck. All lights had been extinguished, and he groped ahead blindly. Unaware of the catastrophe unfolding above him Nikolai recalls marveling at the increasing realism of the night damage-control drills. He arrived at his battle station in time to start the huge diesel generator before five other stunned shipmates joined him. His crew was able to restore lighting quickly throughout most aft portions of the ship. Keeping his generator on line for more than two and a half hours, he provided urgently needed emergency lighting. A little after 4:00 a.m. Nikolai suddenly felt the ship lurch to port. After a shuddering pause, to his horror, the ship began to roll over. The engineers struggled to keep their footing, but Nikolai fell, bashing his head on his beloved engine and badly wrenching his leg on a pipe as his world suddenly turned upside down.

Nikolai awoke neck-deep in water, with the hot engine hanging from the floor plates above his head. Water rushed in through the access hatch, now deep below him, leaving an air pocket above his head extending three feet to the bilges. The engine ground to a stop, and Nikolai froze as if in a dream, waiting for his life to end. The emergency battle lanterns, now the only source of light, began to sputter and then died out, casting the compartment into a pall of darkness. The only sound was water dripping and hissing from the sides of the hot diesel generator.

Nikolai began to call out for his shipmates. Five sailors answered his call and splashed toward the sound of his voice. In the total blackness Nikolai began to track the piping to the skin of the hull above his head. Time had no meaning. He knew hours must have passed since the first blast had torn through the ship. He had to find an access through the hull. Several attempts to dive below to exit the dark engine room resulted in near disaster when he ran out of air before even gaining the next level. Nikolai was also becoming confused and increasingly fatigued from the poor-quality air he now shared with five shipmates. He was determined to escape.

Nikolai thought of the different hull openings that might be big enough to crawl through. First he considered the main condenser injection and exhaust, a huge pipe, but that was located in the main engine room two spaces aft. Then he remembered the diesel cooling water overboard discharge had a pipe 400mm in diameter. He found the cooling water line by running his hands along the base of the engine and then up around the water pump to the point where the line discharged the cooling water into the sea. He knew from a recent dry-docking that the thick hull armor always stopped several centimeters from the overboard discharges, and that the hull was weakest there.

Nikolai took a wrench from his pocket, smoothly disconnected the elbow of the line, and slipped his head and shoulders into the pipe. Barely fitting inside, he signaled to his mates. They opened the first valve, and Nikolai climbed farther inside the pipe, an act of considerable difficulty even in the best circumstances.

The pipe was just big enough for his shoulders to squeeze through, but it was stifling and began to compress him like a vise. Once fully inside, he groped for the second valve. He felt ahead with an outstretched arm and found the second valve stop—in the closed position. Now it was the only single moveable object between him and freedom.

He shouted to his mates to crank it open slowly. As soon as it was cracked slightly, though, water smashed into his face, threatening to blast him back inside the pitch black compartment. Fearing that the gushing water would completely flood the compartment and displace their remaining precious air, the sailors closed the valve quickly. Nikolai backed slowly out of the pipe, discouraged. He stood quietly for a moment and suddenly, in frustration, he began striking the hull above him with the wrench. On and on he swung with the deafening blows, fighting the urge to lie down and sleep—realizing the oxygen in the air pocket trapped above him was running out.

Nearly in complete despair, Nikolai suddenly heard an echo. He stopped swinging the wrench and listened. He heard it again. Someone was tapping on the outside of the hull. He had no idea how much time had elapsed since his world turned topsy-turvy, but he forced himself to swing the wrench again, desperately fighting off fatigue. Finally, after fading in and then out of what seemed like a dark tunnel, Nikolai thought he smelled hot burning metal. He forced himself to look up in the darkness toward the bilge. He suddenly saw a red glow. He watched it, mesmerized, as it grew and began to form a line, then gradually a circle, just big enough, he thought to fit his shoulders. Nikolai watched, unable to speak, until the circle was transformed into open blue sky above.

"We're free," he screamed at the top of his lungs.

Nikolai groped in the new shadowy light of the compartment until he found the hand of the nearest mate. Forming a chain, the men began to climb toward the light. They eventually emerged onto the slimy, barnacle-encrusted hull, where strong arms from a knot of waiting rescuers pulled them one by one from the dark abyss. Miraculously, a seventh figure they had neither seen nor heard inside the hull followed them out into the blinding afternoon Sevastopol sunshine. Two more crewmen were eventually rescued by divers who entered the hull from the depths. The rescuers crawled through one dark, flooded passageway after another until they found two nearly drowned sailors still alive. Still, only nine were pulled from the wreck—and those a full two days following the capsizing. The remaining 608 bodies were recovered only after the ship was raised the following year.

The cause of the sinking will probably never be determined. Some suspected Italian "frogmen." Others thought the cause was leftover German bottom mines or explosives planted aboard in machinery before the ship was transferred from Italy. The sinking resulted in a much-delayed review of damage-control procedures and spurred charges and countercharges of poor leadership, lack of familiarity with a foreign-built ship, and most damaging, the suppression of information that could help prevent future accidents. The episode also demonstrated the Russian sailor's courage and resourcefulness in the face of disaster, a quality sailors in coming decades would show time and again.

★ ★ ★

REGARDLESS OF THE CAUSE, the *Novorossysk* disaster will be remembered most as a symbol of the demise of the conventional all-gun surface warship of the Soviet Navy. The immediate result of the sinking was the demotion of navy commander in chief, Nikolai Kuznetsov and his replacement by a new chief. Admiral of the Fleet, twice Hero of the Soviet Union Sergei G. Gorshkov became the father of the modern Soviet Navy. During a 27-year reign, he oversaw a massive revolution in naval doctrine and the construction of a modern, blue-water navy of missile-equipped surface ships and nuclear-powered submarines. Gorshkov, who joined the navy at age 17, became an admiral at age 31. His rapid rise was due largely to his brilliance as a naval commander during the Great Patriotic War. He emerged from the world war one of the few senior Soviet naval heroes, mostly due to his actions during a campaign in Odessa and as commander of the Danube River Flotilla.

In an abrupt reversal of Stalin's post-war expansion plans, Khrushchev directed a halt to further construction of the large surface warships. He commanded the Soviet Navy to scrap all pre-World War II battleships, cruisers, and most of the large ships acquired as German and Italian naval war reparations. According to the non-sailor Khrushchev: "Navy surface ships are good only for carrying heads of state on official visits; they have outlived their time. They're good only as missile platforms."

Khrushchev redirected a defensive strategy anchored on a strong submarine force and a surface fleet restricted to coastal defense of the flanks of a massive ground army. With the support of his defense chief, the celebrated army commander Marshal Georgi Zhukov, he sought to cut costs of new military construction while retaining a gigantic land force. Expenditures for new naval building were drastically cut. As a result, by 1957 the Soviet Navy was reduced from nearly one million men to a force of less than 500,000; more than 350 out of 600 ships were mothballed. In 1955 the U.S.S.R. had produced 81 new submarines and, with their production capacity still increasing, could have exceeded 100 per year had Khrushchev not decided to curtail naval building.

The new navy chief Gorshkov proceeded with the disposal of obsolete battleships and older cruisers following Khrushchev's dictum and stopped building plans for the new, heavy, 36,000-ton *Stalingrad* cruisers, scrapping many of the unfinished hulls on the ways. The building of the Project 68 *Sverdlov* class cruisers was ended after only 14 of the planned 24 were completed. This proved the death knell for large surface ships. The cuts were accompanied by a controversial debate on the value of a conventional surface navy dominated by cruisers. In addition, the large diesel-attack-submarine construction program was also reduced to make way for building better submarines with more sophisticated capabilities.

In 1962 in Leningrad, during the height of the Cuban missile crisis, the mercurial Khrushchev reproached Admiral Gorshkov while they searched frantically for appropriate armed surface ships and high-speed submarine escorts for their merchant ships being challenged en route to Cuba.

"We need ships with autonomy and long range as escorts to Cuba," roared the angry Khrushchev. "How could you be without any?"

"But, sir," replied Gorshkov, "you ordered them all destroyed."

"I ordered no such thing," countered the general secretary.

As the Cold War race to build ballistic missiles heated up, a separate race was already under way to develop nuclear submarines. The U.S. successfully launched the U.S.S. *Nautilus* in 1956, and the Soviet Union followed by launching their first atomic submarine in 1958. The first U.S. Polaris ballistic missile submarine was already operational when, in 1959, the Soviet's launched their first nuclear-powered missile submarine, the *K-19*. By this time the Soviet Navy already had a dozen diesel-powered submarines carrying surface-launched ballistic missiles with a range of 350 miles, a distance requiring the submarine to patrol within range of America's considerable antisubmarine defenses. Yet these subs were no match for the American *Polaris* boats, which could launch missiles while still submerged under the sea, with a range of 1,500 miles, a distance well outside the Soviets' antisubmarine forces. The superiority of Western antisubmarine detection, and destruction abilities, made the goal of obtaining longer range ballistic missiles essential to the Soviet submarine as was its ability to launch missiles while submerged to lessen the risk of detection.

When the Cuban missile crisis erupted in October 1962, the Soviets had few seaworthy nuclear submarines. Most were in shipyards being retrofitted with safer atomic reactors following the accidents suffered aboard the *K-8* and *K-19*. The Russians designated their submarines according to their cruising ranges, and a "K" class submarine was nuclear-powered with unlimited range. Khrushchev's plan to covertly place medium-range ballistic missiles in Cuba had included a plan to station seven ballistic missile submarines in the port of Mariel, Cuba. The secret naval plan, called Operation *Kama*, was forced to use only diesel-powered missile boats because of the lack of capable nuclear-powered units. When the overall plan in Cuba was exposed and thwarted, it proved that the Soviet Union, although leading in the size and throw weight of its rockets, was woefully behind the U.S. in the number and accuracy of long-range strategic missiles and the ability to project significant naval power far from its shores. The Cuban debacle helped set off an accelerated race to launch large numbers of nuclear submarines.

Accidents occur in all navies. Taking large numbers of complex submarines packed with weapons and men to sea is an inherently dangerous business. The Soviet system, however, with a centrally planned and controlled economy, and strict secrecy in all military matters, exacerbated an already accident-fraught enterprise. Immense pressure was put on the navy from the Communist Party Central Committee in Moscow and its economic planners. These directorates imposed unrealistic requirements on the shipbuilding and atomic energy ministries and the navy to meet goals set in five- and ten-year economic plans. We now know that party officials and naval construction leaders falsified records to show compliance with these impossible goals. Nuclear engineering work was undertaken with little or no quality control, and shipyard safety during construction was minimal. Personal advancement was based on meeting production quotas. Throughout the Cold War period, and still in today's Russia, ships were sent to sea with minimal attention to living conditions and safety of the crew.

As the Cold War military competition accelerated, the Soviet Navy began to send its ships and submarines into seas once unfamiliar to Soviet forces. Patrols into the Mediterranean Sea, the Indian Ocean, and the far reaches of the Pacific and Atlantic became routine. But while the navy was operating in new and bigger territories, it was never able to compete with Western navies in terms of a fleet that was balanced overall. Although Russian fleets made significant improvements to their submarine forces, and eventually produced submarines comparable to those of the West in firepower and stealth, they were never able to challenge the fleet air superiority possessed by Western navies. The Soviets remained largely unable to project air power against other ships, or targets ashore, and could not compete in anti-submarine warfare.

The Soviet fear of always lagging behind would play an important role in their naval strategy and would have disasterous consequences. In their constant push to hurry ahead, to put themselves on an equal footing with the West, mistakes were bound to happen, and they knew these mistakes would happen with frightening regularity. In a system where the common good was placed ahead of individual rights, the lack of prudent safeguards for their sailors contributed to the long history of serious accidents.

═══════

CHAPTER TWO

A SUBMARINE IS NOTHING MORE than a long, horizontal steel cylinder, or *pressure hull*, containing power-plant machinery, weapons, sensors, ship control equipment, crew, and life-support equipment. The hull must be strong enough to withstand the crushing pressure of the sea while the ship is submerged. A fairwater or *sail* on top of the submarine's hull provides a streamlined housing for the periscopes and the forest of retractable masts and antennas rising out of the hull. When the ship is submerged at a shallow depth, the crew can raise these various masts and antennas above the water to communicate and to gather information visually through the periscopes and electronically with radar and passive electronic sensors.

One of these masts, called a *snorkel*, allows the submarine to bring in fresh air and to run its diesel engines while remaining submerged. Working from plans captured when they overran

Holland in 1940, the Germans perfected the snorkel system during World War II. The mast contains a large *induction* pipe through which fresh air is drawn into the boat and an *exhaust* pipe that routes either diesel exhaust gases or stale air from the ship back up to be ejected just beneath the surface of the water. Atop the induction pipe is the *head valve*, a special flapper valve that closes automatically whenever waves wash over the mast in order to prevent seawater from rushing into the submarine.

Perched atop the sail, as much as 40 feet above the pressure hull, is a small conning *cockpit* or *bridge*. In modern submarines this cockpit has streamlined doors that close it off to make the top of the sail smooth while the submarine is submerged. Standing on platforms in this cockpit, the *conning officer* (who is the officer directing the ship's motion) and the lookouts can see clearly all around the ship. This is particularly important when maneuvering in restricted waters, such as when entering or leaving port.

Older submarines have a *conning tower*, a sort of miniature pressure hull, inside the base of the sail. Inside the conning tower are the periscope stands for those looking through periscopes, a remote helm station, a small chart table for navigation, and fire control equipment. It was from the conning tower that submarine commanders conducted their attacks against surface ships in World War II. Newer submarines do not have conning towers. The periscope stands, fire control systems, and navigation tables are now housed in the main pressure hull in order to make the hull more streamlined and to enable the hull to withstand greater pressure.

When the submarine is running on the surface, a watch team will man the bridge, and, in restricted waters, the captain normally will join them there. The watch team is headed by a watch officer, who usually is also the conning officer, and who acts for the ship's captain when the captain is not present. (In the United States, this officer is called the officer of the deck.) In addition to one or two lookouts, there are additional watchstanders who communicate via sound-powered phones and interior communications relay systems with the watchstanders in the central command post some 40 feet below inside the pressure hull directly beneath the sail.

The *central command post*, or *CCP*, is the brain of the submarine. The CCP is little larger than the bathroom in an average American home, or, in larger submarines, may be the size of a small living room. All the ship's internal communications systems are available in the CCP, and every few feet microphones dangle from the overhead for the captain or watch officer to use to send commands throughout the submarine. The bulkheads are lined with panels sporting a daunting array of dials and gauges and lights and indicators, all of which taken together by the trained eye reveal the status of the ship and her systems at a glance. The key watchstanders who manually operate the ship control systems, direct the ship's propulsion systems, and operate the ship's fire control systems sit or stand before these panels. There is the *helmsman* who operates the rudders and thus controls the boat's heading. There are the *planesmen* who operate the ship's diving planes to control the ship's depth while submerged. The ship's *diving officer* is responsible for adjusting the ship's *trim* or balance while submerged. In small vestibules just off the command post, yet directly accessible, are the sonar and radar operators, a navigator's representative, a signalman, and the watch engineer, who is responsible for monitoring the ship's propulsion systems. These crew members are controlled by the captain during key moments, or, in his absence, around the clock by the watch officer.

For safety reasons, a submarine is divided into compartments, numbered from bow to stern, which are separated from each other by strong steel bulkheads capable of withstanding the full pressure of being submerged on one side and atmospheric pressure on the other. Passage through these bulkheads is via heavy watertight doors that allow the compartments to be sealed off from one another. Most Soviet diesel submarines generally had six or seven compartments, while nuclear submarines were divided into as many as ten compartments. The air pressure inside each compartment can be controlled to prevent fire or flooding from spreading into a compartment from adjacent compartments. Within each compartment are either two or three decks, with vertical ladders leading to hatches to provide access between the decks.

In order to balance the ship fore and aft, the weight of the major components has to be distributed evenly along the submarine's length, both in the surfaced condition and in the submerged condition. Thus the position of the heavy components, such as the lead-acid batteries, the diesel engines, the nuclear reactors with their massive shielding, and the ship's turbines and reduction gearing usually is determined by their weights. In addition, propulsion equipment has to be located aft, so that it can be connected to the propeller shafts that drive the ship. This generally results in a fairly typical layout in submarines.

For diesel submarines, the heavy engines are generally placed just aft of the midships point, with the generators and motors farther aft so they can be connected to the propeller shafts. The heavy lead-acid batteries are placed farther forward so their weight can counterbalance the weight of the propulsion system aft.

In nuclear submarines, the reactors are the heaviest part of the ship by far. These normally are placed as close to amidships as feasible, and in most cases the propulsion turbines and ship's service turbogenerators are placed farther aft. As with diesel submarines, the weight of the heavy lead-acid storage batteries is placed forward to help offset the weight of the propulsion plant aft.

In missile submarines, the missile compartment, with its strong steel silos, missile launch systems, and heavy missiles was simply placed amidships. This was done by inserting the missile compartment just forward of the reactor compartment in nuclear submarines, and just forward of the diesel engines in a diesel submarine.

Finally, the designers install *variable ballast tanks* or *trim tanks* at each end of the ship and amidships so that seawater may be flooded in or pumped or blown out as needed to keep the ship in balance, or trimmed, both while on the surface and while submerged. These trim tanks also allow the ship's operators to compensate for weight changes caused by using stores and fuel or by changes in levels in the freshwater tanks, and to compensate for buoyancy changes caused by changes in the temperature and salinity of the surrounding seawater. Through the use of the trim system, the operators can achieve neutral buoyancy, with the ship neither heavier nor lighter than the water it is displacing, and can achieve neutral fore-and-aft trim, so that the ship rides on an even keel.

Working from the bow toward the stern is Compartment One, called the *torpedo room*, which can house as many as eight torpedo tubes for launching torpedoes against surface ships or other submarines. (If the submarine has torpedo tubes in the stern, then this compartment is called the *forward torpedo room*, and the aftmost compartment is called the *after torpedo room*.) The tubes have outer and inner doors, which can be operated remotely from inside the submarine. Sailors load a torpedo inside the tube via the inner door, shut the inner door, and prior to launching, flood the tube to equalize the inside pressure with outside sea pressure. The torpedo is launched by opening the outer door, then ejecting the weapon hydraulically, or with high-pressure air, or by using the torpedo's own propulsion energy ("swim-out"). Spare torpedoes are stored in racks just aft of and within easy access of the launching tubes. These same racks usually provide platforms for bunks for as many as 20 or more men who sleep over, under, and around the torpedoes to make maximum use of this large compartment. There are generally a dozen watch-standers in this compartment and many off-watch crewmen sleeping in the bunks around the clock.

Compartment Two usually houses the battery banks on the lower level in tiers. The batteries are arranged in banks of as many as 100 to 150 cells for running the electric motors and providing electric power for lighting and ship's systems. The motors propel the submarine beneath the sea when the main turbines in a nuclear boat, or the diesel engines in a diesel boat, are not in use. Above the batteries are individual cabins for officers, and damage control and equipment spaces. The sonar spaces are often located in Compartment Two as well.

Except in a few cases, Compartment Three is directly beneath the sail and houses the central command post. Above the command post can be seen the very noticeable trunk with a steel ladder leading via two hatches to the sail, then upwards through the inside of the sail to the conning cockpit. These hatches provide access through the pressure hull into the outer sail, which, of course, floods with seawater any time the submarine is submerged. The officers and men of the conning watch clamber up through these two hatches after the submarine surfaces and descend through and shut them when diving from the sea surface.

The next compartment aft, Compartment Four, in a ballistic missile submarine will house the missile silos. This compartment is divided into levels in which other spaces such as a radio room, a dispensary or sick bay, sonar, and other cabins for senior crewmen are located. The missiles can be quite tall, and their silos can reach the entire height of the compartment. In early Soviet missile submarines, like the K-19, the additional height of the missile silos was accommodated by incorporating them into the after portion of the sail, which made the sail much longer than those of other submarines. The sail acted to smooth the flow of water around the missile tubes, thus reducing drag and making the submarine quieter.

The K-19 was the first Soviet nuclear-powered submarine built to carry ballistic missiles. 375-feet long and 4,500 tons, the submarine was capable of speeds up to 26 knots. The first of the Hotel class, K-19 was launched in April 1959 and commissioned by Captain Nikolai Zateyev in November 1960. The K-19 was designed with the capability of striking strategic U.S. targets with atomic-tipped missiles.

At the machinery spaces, the compartmentation schemes varied considerably. The main goal of the designers was to try to position the weight of the reactors as near to amidships as possible. Aboard K-19, Compartment Five housed the diesel generator and various auxiliary machinery, such as air-conditioning equipment, pumps, high-pressure air compressors, evaporators, and damage-control and firefighting equipment.

Compartment Six in nuclear submarines like the K-19 contains the massive reactors in a shielded capsule in the lower half of the compartment. The upper spaces above the shielded reactors have access and monitoring positions for engineers to control the reactor, pumps and associated equipment for ensuring the continuous flow of the reactor liquid coolant, and steam generators for producing the steam to run the turbines.

SUBMARINE CUT-AWAY PLAN OF UPPER DECK

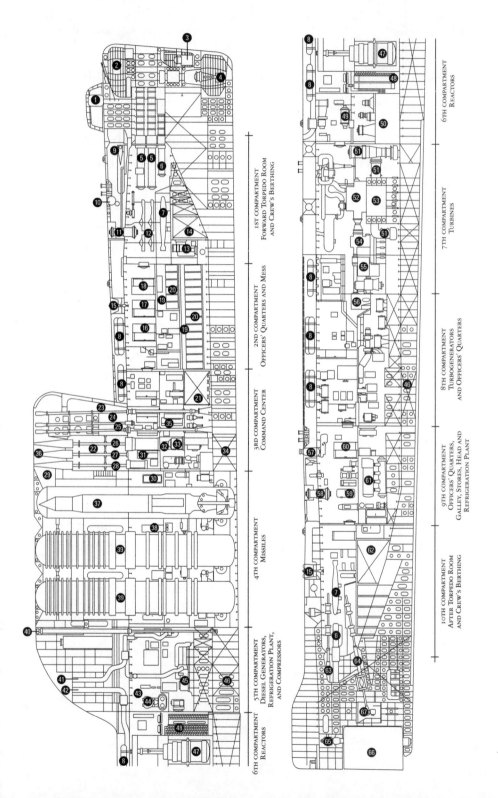

1ST COMPARTMENT
FORWARD TORPEDO ROOM
AND CREW'S BERTHING

2ND COMPARTMENT
OFFICERS' QUARTERS AND MESS

3RD COMPARTMENT
COMMAND CENTER

4TH COMPARTMENT
MISSILES

5TH COMPARTMENT
DIESEL GENERATORS,
REFRIGERATION PLANT,
AND COMPRESSORS

6TH COMPARTMENT
REACTORS

6TH COMPARTMENT
REACTORS

7TH COMPARTMENT
TURBINES

8TH COMPARTMENT
TURBOGENERATORS
AND OFFICERS' QUARTERS

9TH COMPARTMENT
OFFICERS' QUARTERS,
GALLEY, STORES, HEAD AND
REFRIGERATION PLANT

10TH COMPARTMENT
AFTER TORPEDO ROOM
AND CREW'S BERTHING

CUT-AWAY KEY

1. MG-25 active sonar
2. Pluton-658 navigational sonar
3. MG-10 passive sonar
4. Arktika–M (MG-200) sonar
5. 533-mm torpedo tubes (4)
6. 46-mm torpedo tubes (2 forward, 2 aft)
7. Spare 406-mm torpedo
8. Compressed air flasks (410 liters each)
9. Bow planes
10. Anchor windlass
11. Forward escape trunk
12. Bunks
13. Bilge pump 2P-1
14. Forward Trim Tank
15. Emergency signal buoy
16. Two-man officers' stateroom
17. Captain's cabin
18. Four-man officer's stateroom
19. Battery compartment
20. Batteries (Type 38SM)
21. Variable Ballast Tank
22. Conning tower
23. Albatross System (navigation)
24. PR-1 System
25. Nakat electronic surveillance measures (ESM) system
26. PENG-8 periscope
27. PEN-7 periscope
28. RKP system
29. Cockpit
30. Crypto room
31. Sonar room
32. Radar room
33. Gyroscope station
34. Ballast Tanks
35. Radio shack
36. Periscope glands
37. SS-N-4 "Sark," single-warhead missile
38. Doctor's cabin
39. Missile silo for R-13 missile, the *K-19* original ballistic missile type
40. Snorkle Induction Mast
41. Ventilation Exhaust Line
42. Snorkel Exhaust Line
43. Refrigeration plant E-250
44. Evaporators IKV-5/0.63 (for distilling fresh water from sea water)
45. Diesel generator DG-460
46. Main Ballast Tanks
47. Reactors VM-A—2 reactors at 70 MWt (megawatts thermal) each
48. Reactor Shielding
49. Current transformer SPT-75
50. Heat exchangers VP2-1-0 (also referred to as steam generators)
51. Main Seawater Pump
52. Turbine
53. Main Condenser
54. Main reduction gear
55. Main propulsion control
56. Lock chamber platform
57. Capstan
58. After Escape Trunk
59. Galley
60. Twelve-man mess
61. Air conditioning unit E-320
62. After Trim Tank
63. Rudder ram
64. Stern Planes ram
65. Rudder head
66. Rudder
67. Stern Planes activator

The engineering equipment, including the steam turbines, is housed in Compartment Seven, with the electric drive motors, or *main motors*, located in Compartment Eight. The main propeller shafts extend aft from Compartment Eight, penetrating each of the engineering space bulkheads through flexible glands that seal the shafts to preserve compartment integrity. These shafts, about level with the ship's mid-plane, pass through the last two compartments, Nine and Ten, and then pass through the pressure hull via adjustable packing glands called *shaft seals*. At the after end of the shafts are the propellers that provide the submarine's motive power. Compartment Nine has crew quarters, the crew's galley, the sick bay, and the air-conditioning plant, while Compartment Ten has more crew quarters and storerooms for provisions, plus the operating mechanisms for the rudder and stern planes.

The submarine has emergency escape trunks with double hatches located above the next-to-last compartment and the forward torpedo compartment, thus providing three accesses through the hull, one at each end of the ship and the one from Compartment Three leading from the central command post to the upper sail. These escape trunks have upper and lower hatches, and thus can be used as airlocks to leave the ship in an emergency. There are additional crew berths scattered throughout the submarine, and normally in Russian submarines the crew's dining and leisure spaces are located in one of the after engineering compartments. Each compartment of a Russian submarine has an officer designated in charge. That officer is responsible for the material condition of his compartment and acts as the senior in charge in case of fire and flooding in his spaces.

Although generally austere in nature, life aboard submarines is highly challenging and often rewarding. In modern Russian submarines there are exercise rooms, a space for watching films, saunas, and smoking vestibules for off-watch crewmen. The Typhoon-class submarines even have small swimming pools!

Since the volume of a submarine's pressure hull displaces just slightly less than its own weight in water, and thus would be right at the surface, an outer hull, made of weaker material, encases the pressure hull and provides it with additional buoyancy so that on the surface the submarine will ride higher out of the water. This outer hull or *casing* increases the total volume of the submarine without adding significantly to its weight. The space between the outer casing and the pressure hull is divided into tanks, which hold fuel for diesel boats, fresh water, and the main ballast tanks. The main ballast tanks are filled with air when the submarine is surfaced and are filled with seawater when the submarine submerges. While it is on the surface, only about one-seventh of a submarine's volume is above water level. Upon submerging, the ship is trimmed by admitting water to or pumping water from the variable ballast tanks until the submarine is neutrally buoyant. Water is pumped back and forth between tanks to adjust the fore-and-aft trim of the boat. Once trimmed, the submarine reaches and maintains its desired depth using a combination of the angle of the ship (pitch control) and speed. Small movable control surfaces called *diving planes* are used much like the control surfaces of an aircraft. While submerged, the forward surfaces, fixed to the bow (*bow planes*) or on the sail (*sail planes*), are used primarily to control the ship's depth, while the after surfaces at the stern of the ship (*stern planes*) are used primarily to control the ship's angle. The three-dimensional motion of submerged submarines is similar to that of an airplane.

Since the submarine is designed for cruising underwater, it has very little reserve buoyancy when on the surface, and pressure hull damage may prove fatal. A surface ship displacing an equal number of tons as a submarine enjoys considerably more reserve buoyancy and can absorb considerable damage, taking aboard water up to her total weight before sinking. A surfaced submarine, however, can ship aboard only about a fifth of her weight of seawater before becoming in danger of sinking. Since the submarine's fittings, engines, batteries, and equipment are compacted within a severely limited space, repairs of any kind are extremely complex. So, whereas a surface warship like a destroyer can be saved from extensive battle damage by repairing the hull, a submarine with pressure hull damage may well be doomed to a crushing plunge to the depths of the ocean. Life aboard a submarine is precarious at best.

★ ★ ★

A RUSSIAN SUBMARINE IS DIVIDED into numbered divisions much like the departments of U.S. ships: operations and navigation, communications and electronics, weapons, missiles and torpedoes, engineering, and damage control. In the Soviet period the submarine captain had a number of assistants called deputy commanders. His senior deputy, the *starpom*, called the executive officer in the West, was the second in command and generally backed up the captain in all functions. The deputy commander for political affairs, the *zampolit*, was in charge of political doctrine, morale, and welfare. The deputy for security was the officer in charge of counterintelligence, personnel security, and safety of nuclear weapons. During the early days of nuclear power the political officer wielded a great deal of clout, but as nuclear weapons became more numerous, his authority was supplanted by the deputy for security.

The watch officer positions aboard submarines, such as navigator, weapons, antisubmarine warfare, torpedo, and communications, were usually limited to the six most experienced officers. They held the most demanding positions, that of conning the submarines for the commanding officer. These men stood duties as watch officers in addition to their normal assignments.

There are more officers aboard Russian submarines than aboard their American counterparts. This is primarily because the Russians lack the strong senior petty officer system of the U.S. Navy. Jobs normally held by senior enlisted and chief petty officers in the American submarine service, such as sonar technician, radioman, electrician's mate, and quartermaster are held by officers in the Soviet Navy. Thus aboard a nuclear submarine in the Russian navy with a total crew of 100 men, there could be as many as 30 officers, whereas aboard a similar size American submarine the ratio would be closer to 15 officers.

Enormous gaps still exist in the known history of the Soviet Navy, especially within the submarine force. In these gaps lie not only design and command blunders, but also numerous accounts of courage and extraordinary heroism sailors' displayed when ships exploded, burned, and collapsed around them. Until the new openness of the Gorbachev era of the late 1980s, all serious naval accidents were concealed on the orders of the Supreme Soviet. In the Russian fleet today, the younger generation of sailors is still not fully aware of the full scale of the early accidents.

★ ★ ★

ON THE EVENING OF NOVEMBER 21, 1956, a year after the loss of the battleship *Novorossysk*, tragedy struck the Soviet Navy again in the rough waters of the Baltic Sea. At 7:40 p.m. the watch officer aboard Baltic Fleet destroyer *Statnyi* reported to commanding officer Captain Third Rank Yu. S. Samchuk a surface contact barely visible in the early darkness. The contact lay dead ahead in the narrow channel approaches to Paldisky near the city of Tallinn, Estonia. After tracking the intermittent contact on radar, the watch officer grew uneasy and finally requested the presence of the commanding officer on the bridge. He reported that he was unsure of the track of the contact, because it was small, but it appeared to be heading toward the destroyer in the middle of the channel. The report was the correct move by any watch officer unsure of a developing situation.

The stormy weather was normal for the Baltic Sea, with 30 knot winds and poor visibility due to intermittent rain squalls. The Baltic has long had a reputation for being difficult for any sailor. Captain Samchuk, standing on the bridge of the destroyer, strained his eyes into the evening rain.

"What's her bearing drift?"

"Steady bearing, decreasing range, Comrade Commander."

"Hug the right side of the channel for a port-to-port passing, and try not to run aground."

"Aye, Comrade Commander." The watch officer squinted through the binoculars, then turned to the helmsman. "Come right to new course 045, decrease turns to ten knots."

"Aye sir, coming right to new course 045, indicating turns for ten knots. Engine room answers, 52 rpm for ten knots."

As the two officers stood side by side, the faint smell of the swampy shoreline intermingled with the salt water of the autumn Baltic. The cold wind stabbed through their standard navy-issue foul-weather jackets, which never seemed to keep out the cold.

"I hold her coming straight toward us, showing red and green running lights together, straight down the throat."

"Slow more and stand by to give some signals," the young commanding officer growled, hoping not to sound panicky, although it was his first time bringing the ship through the tricky straits at night.

Samchuk was from Kiev and tried hard not to let his Ukrainian accent show when speaking with his officers, especially if they were obviously Russians from the north. They seemed to take to the natural hardships of the Baltic and Northern Fleet conditions much better than those from the southern regions of the Soviet Union. Samchuk, a graduate of the Higher Naval School in Baku, was conscious of the arrogance of the Leningrad-trained officers

Two hundred meters ahead, aboard the small diesel submarine *M-200 Malyutka*, Captain Third Rank A. S. Shumanin peered from the open cockpit atop his conning tower on the sail. Two lookouts and a watch officer stood jammed inside the cockpit with the young captain, all straining to see through the wind-driven rain. This was the worst part of the narrow channel, not a comfortable position for a captain returning his submarine from his first patrol since he took command on November 18, three long days ago. He still had not had time to report to the division commander before taking his submarine out on a scheduled exercise in the area west of Tallinn. He had to get this wallowing ancient hulk safely back to port before doing that.

The submarine, one of the small 27-man *Malyutka* series, had been built during World War II and had served throughout the war years in the north out of Polyarny, a small fishing village turned submarine base in the Kola Peninsula north of Murmansk. In an effort to extend these diesel submarines' cruising range, a stopgap before the first nuclear-powered submarines became operational, liquid oxygen had been introduced to allow these submarines to run their diesel engines while submerged. The new design proved a serious explosion and fire hazard, earning the submarines the nickname "cigarette lighters." After fitting out with the new experimental diesel engines, *M-200* had been transferred to the Baltic, making her home port in Paldisky, outside Tallinn, one of the most sought-after home ports of the Soviet Navy. In the Estonian port sailors lived better, ate better, and generally fared better in all respects than in the frigid ports scattered along the Kola Peninsula in the far north. Also they had only rain and chop to contend with at sea rather than blizzards, white outs, and the awful ice.

The submarine was expecting to pass an outbound destroyer in midchannel. Looking for the approaching destroyer, Captain Shumanin strained to see through his useless glasses, leaned down to wipe the lenses for the hundredth time, cursing the rain.

"Contact dead ahead, closing fast!" the lookout cried suddenly. He raised his arm in a futile gesture, as if to fend off the towering stem of the destroyer heading on a collision course. Shumanin looked up immediately and froze. His bowels loosened as he watched the black outline of a destroyer bow loom within a meter of his navigation cockpit. For a moment he was unable to give a command—what command could make a difference at this point? He closed his eyes against the impending catastrophe.

"All back full!" he managed to get out to the lee helmsman just before the stem of the destroyer sliced through his submarine's hull aft of the conning tower. The tremendous impact threw all six men, including the captain, out of the cockpit. Six minutes earlier, the Brigade Chief of Staff had left the bridge to go below for dinner; he never came up again.

The destroyer's stem cut directly into the submarine's Compartment Six, killing six men immediately. The submarine's bow flooded immediately, and she briefly hung vertically before sinking, while all those located in the bridge cockpit jumped free. Within 20 minutes, six men, including the captain, were fished out of the water and rescued aboard the destroyer. Two other seamen who had jumped clear could not be found.

Directly following impact, the collision alarm was sounded aboard destroyer *Statnyi* and crewmen threw life rings to the men they had seen flying from the submarine's open bridge. The destroyer dropped anchor immediately, and while rescuers were bringing in the swimmers from the submarine's crew, repair parties made temporary repairs to the destroyer's bow. They built a temporary patch from mattresses strengthened by wooden shoring to stop most of the leaking. The commanding officer of the destroyer took over and organized the search for the sunken submarine. Within minutes after the collision, 33 different navy ships began to gather at the scene, including the cruiser *Zhdanov*, two submarines, a large antisubmarine ship, and five trawlers and rescue ships. The antisubmarine vessel, *SO-185*, managed to locate the sunken hull and established underwater communications with the trapped crewmen using her own and the destroyer's underwater hydro-acoustic telephones. The rescuers were able to speak with the submarine's second in command, Lieutenant V. Kolpakova, who reported that there were still six men alive, trapped in the bow compartment of the submarine.

After some time, Kolpakova was able to communicate with Compartment Three, the central command post, and determined that some crewmen were still alive there as well. Soon, however, chlorine gas, released when seawater flooded the battery cells, filled that section of the boat and killed all who remained.

The submarine was resting 55 meters down, but the depth meter in the bow where the six remained alive read 35 meters. The executive officer reported the six survivors had found Individual Rescue Devices, which should enable them to escape from the hull. Unfortunately, the commander of the rescue forces, Vice Admiral V. S. Cherkov, initially refused to allow the men to abandon the submarine. He feared by giving permission he would be held responsible for their certain deaths by the bends (a risk to divers who rise to the surface too quickly). Instead, he decided to tow the submarine to shallower waters. The rescue ships, however, were unable to rig an underwater harness.

At 7:00 a.m. on November 22, the admiral gave the order to pump air into the submarine in order to save the crewmen. The men trapped aboard had been awaiting permission to evacuate since 5:00 p.m. the day before. Before giving the order to evacuate, the commander decided to reposition a number of rescue ships. In the process, he lost underwater communications with the submarine. The air in the submarine would last until five the next morning. Finally, at 3:47 a.m., November 23, the men in the downed submarine decided to exit on their own initiative. In the process, the first became lodged in the exit. As a result, all six suffocated.

The *Malyutka* was raised in the beginning of December. Out of a total crew of 27, only the six who were standing watch in the navigation cockpit were saved. The sailors are buried in a communal mausoleum in Paldiski, Estonia.

The tragedy was covered up. The men who died were listed as "missing without a trace" and were not acknowledged to have been lost during an accident. The announcement sent to next of kin merely stated that, "they gave their lives for the "Motherland" but not in "combat." The commanding officer was convicted of personal negligence, forced to retire, and sworn to secrecy concerning the accident.

★ ★ ★

KEY FACTORS THAT WOULD PLAGUE the Soviet submarine force repeatedly in the years ahead were in evidence in another accident less than one year later. On August 22, 1957, another diesel attack submarine suffered an accident in the Cape Feolente training area southwest of Sevastopol in the Black Sea. (The event occurred just a week before a navy Captain Second Rank named Nikolai Zateyev, then serving in the same area aboard a similar submarine, received new secret orders to proceed to the north and take command of the first atomic-powered ballistic missile submarine, the *K-19*.) The unlucky diesel submarine had spent most of the day submerged and at 5:00 p.m. was due to return to port. She failed to show.

Earlier, Commanding Officer Captain Third Rank R. Belozerov, an experienced and highly regarded commander, had given the command for a crash dive as the crew simulated an escape from approaching enemy aircraft. Belozerov had ordered the drill repeatedly to cut the time required for the crew to "crash dive" the boat, that is to clear the bridge, shut the bridge hatches, and flood the main ballast tanks, while simultaneously driving the bow down with the bow planes. After the fifth drill in two hours, the crew had become anxious to complete the exercises and return to port. They grew careless.

"All compartments report," snarled the commander glancing at the chronometer on the navigator's station before shifting his view to the manometer as the depth registered 10, 12, then 20 meters.

The deck plates beneath his feet shuddered as he felt the down angle on the bow drop away. He wanted to break the three-and-a-half-minute record achieved 30 minutes earlier.

Reports came in and were checked off by the watch officer, standing just to the right of the commander.

"Compartment One, manned and ready."

"Compartment Two, all secure."

"Compartment Three—"

Suddenly, out of order, came the cry: "Control, heavy flooding in Compartment Six." Six was the diesel machinery compartment, home of the engineers and the new enriched-oxygen diesel engines. Compartment Six also contained the snorkel induction hull valve, which was notorious for malfunctioning, especially when hasty crewmen spun the control valve wheel too rapidly and the gate didn't close completely, or remained ajar because a bit of flotsam jammed between the valve and the valve seat. Although the remote indicator in the central control post showed the main induction air trunk valve closed, water gushed into Compartment Six. Engineers fought to close the manual quick-close backup valve, but the water was already flowing with a force impossible to stop. The machinery space was plunged into darkness amid sparks and steam as the tremendous flow of cold seawater reacted with the hot diesel casings and shorted the electrical connections. The submarine lost all way. The stern gradually fell until reaching nearly a 60-degree angle down by the stern. It crashed into hard sand at a depth of 40 meters.

The submarine hit bottom with a tremendous shudder that scattered men, equipment, and machinery in all directions. Compartment Six was already half flooded, and water was forcing its way to the aftermost Compartment Seven through a bulkhead sprung by the boat's impact with the bottom. As water reached the live electrical switchboards in Seven, more sparks began to fly. With a sudden blue flash a violent electrical fire ripped through the compartment. Engineers in Compartment Six finally cut all power aft, containing the electrical fire.

Quiet reigned. Stunned crewmen fought to regain their senses. Switching on emergency lighting, they were able to begin to take stock of the situation. The engine room by this time was more than two-thirds flooded, and seawater continued to gush in through the partially open main induction valve.

Captain Belozerov calmly listened to his chief mechanic and realized that Compartments Four and Five were the only ones relatively watertight. Even the central command post in Compartment Three was taking on water. He immediately ordered all hands in the end compartments to Compartment Five.

This was no easy matter. The eight men from the forward torpedo room gathered wide-eyed at the main watertight door leading aft to Compartment Two. Water was already leaking over the coamings around each door from the badly leaking torpedo tubes. The men reported ready, then on signal they wrestled the heavy door open and fought their way aft as quickly as possible. Compartment Two was not safe, either. As seawater reached the large banks of 200 batteries on the middle level, the reaction generated deadly chlorine gas. The crewmen needed to escape this compartment as quickly as possible. Already a thin mist of the deadly gas was starting to curl upward from the battery compartment. The combined complement of Compartments One and Two huddled near the after watertight door, awaiting the command to pass through. The command given, they opened the door and stumbled through into the central command post. To their amazement there was already water on the deck plates, and only the commanding officer and the chief mechanic stood in what was normally the humming brain of the submarine.

The dim light of the battery-powered battle lanterns cast eerie shadows as the men stepped aft through the already open after door into Compartment Four. This compartment stood in total darkness, and the men, carrying the portable lamps, felt their way still farther aft through the crew's mess, the sick bay, medical compartment, officers' berthing, and toward the last door leading to Compartment Five. The door was undamaged, and the crewmen, now numbering 35, stumbled into the dry compartment. The commander and chief mechanic followed the group and made sure the forward hatch into Compartment Five was closed and tightly dogged.

Two hours had passed since the sub had hit bottom, and the commanding officer analyzed the situation. More than 40 tons of seawater had entered the submarine, which still sat at a 60-degree angle down by the stern. There was enough oxygen aboard to last for 70 hours, and enough food and water for two days. The communicators had released the emergency signal buoy, but the crew were uncertain if it had deployed properly.

The use of the emergency buoys was of major concern to the captain. He remembered another submarine in their brigade having been caught tack-welding the expensive and delicate emergency buoys to the hull to prevent their inadvertent loss. Normally they were attached by pressure-sensitive release couplings. Yet several had been lost earlier in heavy seas, deployed their antennae, and emitted the emergency signals, which caused needless havoc and deployment of rescue forces. Instead of regarding the situation as an accident and trying to improve the use and deployment of the buoys, headquarters had cashiered the communications officer and CO as punishment, leading other units to take measures to render their buoys stationary—and thus inoperable in a real emergency.

Captain Belozerov, deciding to reduce the weight in the stern, set up a bucket brigade. Men passed containers of seawater forward by hand from the partially flooded after compartments. The strenuous work caused increased breathing, and the oxygen supply diminished quickly. One by one crewmen began to lose consciousness. They finally stopped the work to conserve the critical air supply.

While the men aboard the downed submarine were fighting to change the trim and lift the stern out of the mud, submarine rescue forces converged at the scene. The emergency signal buoy had worked, and rescuers were able to establish clear communications with the trapped men. The immediate danger to the crew was the extreme cold and the poor air supply. The rescue force commander, Captain First Rank Nikolai Chiker, hurriedly ordered divers to pass a cable under the submarine's bow and try to wrench her free from the bottom using tugs. The rescue ship passed suction hoses down to help empty the flooded compartments, and divers descended carrying warm clothing and emergency rations, which they passed through the torpedo tube locks to the men inside. By this point, half the available oxygen had been used.

Divers placed the cable under the hull, but the initial towing attempts failed when the towing cable snapped. The rescue effort was postponed by heavy seas, and when a new towing cable was deployed, it too broke. The air supply was now dangerously low. By the early morning hours of August 26, however, nearly 79 hours after the submarine had gone down, she was successfully towed to shallow water. The men inside the submarine had managed to pump out the remaining ballast, and slowly the sub rose to the surface. In an extraordinary display of courage, all the trapped were rescued. Not a single sailor was lost—seven hours after their air should have run out.

★ ★ ★

ANOTHER STARTLING ACCIDENT occurred in early 1961. Few details are known about the event as there were no survivors. The salvage effort following the recovery of the submarine offers an example of the extremes to which the Soviet leadership would go to maintain secrecy at all costs.

Submarine S-80, an experimental diesel-powered boat designed for testing cruise missiles, was lost without a trace, with all hands, on January 27, 1961. The submarine was found five years later in 600 feet of water off the Kola Peninsula. While the salvage forces gathered to raise the hull, NATO reconnaissance aircraft and surface surveillance ships converged at the site. Soviet salvage personnel raised the hull, slung it beneath a large lifting ship, and carried it underwater hundreds of miles to a Kola Gulf fjord where the S-80 could be retrieved out of sight of prying eyes. The submarine was found to have sunk as a result of sudden flooding through a faulty check valve in the snorkel equipment. Snorkeling in northern waters was inherently dangerous because of the high possibilities that ice would form on the submarine's snorkel valve, disabling it.

The remains of 68 crewmen were found inside the ill-fated submarine. All the food aboard had been consumed, and there were signs that the crew had survived for several days before succumbing to carbon-dioxide poisoning. Oxygen was discovered in unused canisters.

CHAPTER THREE

**B**y October 1959, when Captain
Nikolai Zateyev took command of the
newest nuclear-powered ballistic missile
boat in Severodvinsk, the large shipbuilding port near Archangelsk on the
White Sea in northern Russia, the Soviet
Navy was steaming full speed toward the goal of a massive force
of nuclear submarines. At the time, the Americans were already
operating their first atomic submarines. The U.S.S. *Nautilus,*
launched in 1954, had already sailed under the ice of the Arctic
Sea to the North Pole, and the second nuclear-powered submarine, the U.S.S. *Seawolf,* had already been launched. Four Skate-
class nuclear boats were in production in Groton, Connecticut;
Portsmouth, New Hampshire; and at the Mare Island navy shipyard near San Francisco. The Soviet shipbuilding industry was
faced with the task of preventing the Americans from extending their lead in the use of nuclear power in naval warships. Ship-

yards in Severodvinsk, Leningrad on the Baltic, Nikolayev on the Black Sea, and near Vladivostok in the Pacific were building nuclear submarines. Nuclear boats were also being built in Gorky, west of the Ural Mountains on the Volga River, where they were loaded onto floating barges and delivered to the White or Baltic Sea via the extensive inland waterway systems, to ports where they underwent fitting out and sea trials.

A deficit of qualified officers and experienced crewmen became a major obstacle to the rapidly expanding nuclear submarine force. Finding officers who had both command experience and enough savvy to return to basic education in nuclear power was a serious challenge. The difficulty of recruiting trainable and experienced submarine engineers was even greater. Most experienced submarine chief engineers were already older, as they had spent years working their way up to those positions; few had enough time left in the service to be retrained in nuclear power. This led to the acceleration of the training for young engineer officers, who entered the atomic-power program with minimal experience at sea in submarines. Nuclear-powered submarines had steam-driven, turboelectric power plants, and many submarine engineers were recruited from steam turbine-powered surface ships. In this case the only difference was the use of a reactor instead of a fossil fuel, such as oil, as the energy source.

The navy selected Nikolai Zateyev to be the commander of the first atomic-powered strategic missile submarine, the K-19. Filling the key crew positions with qualified officers and senior petty officers was just one of many challenges confronting the new captain.

Captain Second Rank Nikolai Zateyev was born in 1926 and, like many others, his family suffered through the devastation of World War II. The son of a factory worker, young Nikolai was determined to join the navy and gained admittance to the S. M. Kirov Caspian Higher Naval School in Baku, one of the elite naval training academies. He was a brilliant student and soon advanced to submarine training. His first navy years were spent as a young officer in the bleak Northern Fleet in the Kola Gulf, where he served as an officer in diesel submarines. His chosen field was the navigation-operations branch, although he later qualified also as a torpedo and mine officer. His excellent performance aboard two diesel submarines in the north and as a mid-grade officer at the Leningrad Naval Academy (equivalent to the U.S. command and staff course at the Naval War College) soon resulted in his being rewarded with command of his own diesel-powered submarine at the young age of 26. He assumed his first command in the Black Sea Fleet, where he and his wife, Antonina, and daughter lived in the gleaming Crimean port of Sevastopol.

The Soviet armed forces used universal conscription, whereby every young male citizen was required to serve a set number of years in uniform, for a submariner as many as six years, but the term varied with the period and the branch of service. Most navy recruits were, as in the U.S. during the time of the draft, young men who volunteered to serve in the more attractive sea service where life was materially better than in the larger ground forces. In the Soviet system, pay in currency was limited, but sailors received free food, minimal clothing, and limited medical care. Even though access to luxury goods in special navy stores varied with rank and length of service, there was a long waiting line to enter the navy, especially the submarine service. As a result only those with exceptional intelligence or other qualifying background were accepted, raising the quality of young sailors, most of whom hailed from remote villages where life offered little chance for a bright young man to advance beyond his primitive surroundings.

Training for Soviet Navy recruits was similar to that in the West. Basic military training took place at a general training center, followed by specialized training in the branch of choice: engineering, navigation, communications, or weapons. A major difference from Western navy education and training was that a great deal more time was spent indoctrinating the Russian sailor in political loyalty than in esprit de corps. Soviet submariners seldom received cross training. Ensuring that any crewman could take over the function of the next has always been an important element of Western submarine training. Yet Soviet engineers remained solely engineers, and weapons and missile technicians remained strictly in their specialties throughout their careers and learned little of the other fields.

The Soviet naval officer corps was drawn from three basic pools. The first was hardworking students who were highly motivated, better educated, and scored higher on competitive examinations. A second group consisted of young men whose fathers had served with distinction in the forces. The third had parents who belonged to the highly privileged class of the Party and were free to enter the field of their choice.

There are two types of officers with the Soviet Navy. The first learned how to operate ships and were educated in the technical specialties of engineering, weapons, communications, or electronics. The second were political and security officers. Only those in the first category could qualify for command. Those in the political branches were assigned to ships and shore commands as officers called *zampolits*, responsible for political indoctrination, morale, and welfare. Security officers were frequently assigned under the cover of a normal operational position and were responsible for counter-intelligence, personnel, and nuclear weapons security. The political and security officers, called "deputies to the commanding officer," could not succeed to command. They also reported via a separate chain of command to their political and security directorates within the navy.

During World War II, the navy had dispersed its officer training facilities, and ten higher naval schools existed, from Gorky, on the Volga; Baku, on the Caspian Sea; and Sevastopol, on the Black Sea. Soviet Navy Commander in Chief Admiral Kuznetsov had geographically dispersed the training facilities to avoid losing all his young naval officers to the Germans. Although the Leningrad Higher Naval School had never closed, most of the activity of the naval cadets during the siege of 1942-44 was directed for the defense of the city, just to stay alive and feed themselves.

Leaders, from the lowest petty officer to junior and senior officers, were discouraged from thinking independently. Instead they were taught never to exceed their authority, and to operate strictly by the rule book. This exaggerated fear of senior authority, which permeated all the Soviet armed forces, was responsible for the frequent covering up of shortcomings and mistakes. When coupled with a cavalier attitude toward safety, this fear of authority was responsible for many of the accidents that plagued the Russian Navy—and the accident rate increased with the rising complexity of their ships and submarines.

Nikolai Zateyev was a strong commanding officer, yet while he maintained the Party standing required of an officer, he kept his distance from political affairs. Nor did his abiding care for the welfare of his men endear him to the navy leadership, which often brought him into open conflict with the political officers of his fleet staffs. Zateyev, nevertheless, became well known as a highly successful commander who was extremely popular with his men.

His superb record in the Black Sea submarine force while a commander of two diesel submarines made him a prime candidate for the coveted command of a new nuclear-powered submarine.

During his entire career Zateyev kept a meticulous diary, which in his later years he used to compose a memoir. He regularly recorded his thoughts and feelings about the navy, the system, and detailed his experiences. His insights into the life of naval officers, specifically the navy culture, are unique. The most valuable parts concern his experience during the crucial formative years of the atomic submarine force. Zateyev's criticism of the safety of nuclear power in Soviet submarines and in land-based nuclear plants reveals how dangerous the early nuclear plants were. His observations are particularly helpful in explaining how the submarine designers and builders clashed sharply with the sailors, who had to take these new and inadequately tested platforms to sea and to patrol the ocean depths with lethal weapons tucked in beside their own living spaces. His memoir contains the extraordinary account of not only his experiences aboard the *K-19*, and the ordeal of his first nuclear command, but also a scathing indictment of the navy nuclear-power program and shipbuilding industry. Zateyev's critique of the shortcomings proved relevant not only during the Cold War naval arms race, but also throughout the nine-year period following the 1991 fall of the Soviet Empire, and leading to the August 2000 disaster aboard the super-submarine *Kursk*.

Captain Zateyev's concerns, expressed in his own words, clearly define the underlying reasons for many of the accidents and misfortunes suffered by the Soviet fleet. The portions of his memoir reproduced here illustrate the considerable burdens faced by the commanding officers of Soviet nuclear submarines in that era and in the years to come.

★ ★ ★

ON SEPTEMBER 2, 1957, I was summoned to the Navy Department of Personnel. After an in-depth interview with the department head I was offered a transfer to the nuclear fleet as the commander of a submarine armed with ballistic missiles. We knew that our country had begun building nuclear submarines, but our knowledge was fragmentary, based only on rumors. The offer of command of a nuclear submarine came as a total surprise to me, and naturally, it was quite a boost to my ego. But more than anything else it would mean changing a lifestyle that had become more or less stable. It had been less than a year since I'd been given my first government-issued apartment; my daughter had just started school; and there were plenty of other considerations. It also meant changing fleets. I'd be trading the warmth of the Black Sea Fleet for the chill of the Northern. I asked for some time to think it over and consult with my wife.

Thinking it over didn't take much time. My wife, Antonina Aleksandrovna, was willing to go with me wherever we had to go, even if it meant trading the beautiful southern city of Sevastopol for the harsh climate of the Far North or Far East. I went back to the personnel department and gave my consent. I was asked there not to report a single thing to my superiors and not to say anything even to my closest friends.

Our entire family had to spend a week being examined by a medical commission examining specific medical indicators. They had to certify that I was fit for service aboard a nuclear vessel (this involves some special physical qualifications) and that my wife and daughter would be able to tolerate living in the North. An entire week of exams, X-rays, and giving samples of everything you could give samples of. They took a hard look at everything, looking for every possible health problem. To my great relief, we were all pronounced healthy. What more could a man ask? If you're in good health and your family is healthy you're free to live and work to your heart's content!

I didn't tell Antonina, though, that I was transferring to the nuclear fleet. I decided to brief her on my new commission only after my orders were issued. Meanwhile, I told her that the thorough physical, i.e., being processed by the medical commission, was required because submarine *S-98* was being transferred to the North. As I've already mentioned, I had been strictly instructed to keep my transfer to the nuclear fleet a complete secret. Not even my brigade command was notified.

After we'd been through the medical commission, which had certified that I was fit to work with radioactive substances and that my family was fit for life in the North, I reported this to the personnel department. There I was handed long questionnaires, life histories (mine and my wife's), and other documents to fill out, along with instructions on *how* they were to be filled out and what one was supposed to write. I managed to ask Leonid Lysenko, Captain Third Rank of Personnel, in a casual sort of way about my references; after all, I was on pretty bad terms with my superiors. He grinned at that and told me not to worry about it. They selected officers for the nuclear fleet based on proven professional qualifications, not the opinion of any superiors. "As for your particular case," Lysenko went on, "there's no one else in the navy for this job but you. Your commanding officers were instructed to submit both a performance report and a Party reference on you, which they did, although they never knew why these were needed. And both men gave you a positive rating, even a good one." Lysenko advised me to be patient and wait. So I was.

★ ★ ★

SELECTION FOR NUCLEAR SUBMARINE command in the Soviet fleet was carefully controlled by the senior ranks of the fleet's operational and political directorates and the Central Committee of the Communist Party. Although the United States had no political screening, in the U.S. Navy during the early nuclear period, final selection of officers was controlled by Admiral Hyman Rickover, head of the nuclear reactors division of the Chief of Naval Operations staff, considered the father of the atomic submarine program, who embodied all of the equivalent Soviet agencies into one person. Hyman Rickover was a graduate of the U.S. Naval Academy who had worked his way into the unique position of personally directing the selection and training of all personnel in the U.S. Navy's nuclear power program. A stickler for education and dedication to work, his popularity with the U.S. Congress kept him in this top navy position far beyond the time when the navy felt the need for him. Under Rickover's early tutelge all officers were enrolled for two years of formal study in engineering, mathematics, and physics at Union College in Schenectady, New York. Following that, they performed hands-on reactor training at the U.S.S. *Nautilus* land-based prototype nuclear reactor in Idaho Falls, Idaho, or at the U.S.S. *Seawolf* prototype reactor at Ballston Spa, West Milton, New York, before finally attending the navy's formal submarine school at New London, Connecticut. The training was especially inten-

sive for prospective submarine officers and engineering person-·
nel of all ranks. It is no doubt due to the intensity of the training that Rickover designed that the nuclear power safety record
of the U.S. Navy is so superb. Similar but much shorter training
existed in the early days of nuclear power in the Soviet Union.

★ ★ ★

TURNING THE SHIP OVER to the executive officer didn't take
long. But for some reason my superiors were in no hurry to
let me go. For that matter, filling out various forms, reporting to various offices, "booking" an apartment, and so on took
ages. And I myself was in no particular hurry. To be honest,
I was reluctant to part with my ship, and especially with my
crew. I had assembled the kind of team with which I could
go through hell or high water with no hesitation. For better
or worse, I always tried to make good men of my subordinates, to make them competent specialists, skilled and inde-
pendent mentors of their own subordinates, who were for the
most part young seamen or petty officers like themselves. It's
not for me to judge my own merits as a commander and men-
tor. But I know I passed on something positive of myself to
the men in my charge, something that took root in their characters and in their actions. A number of them later became
submarine commanders. For instance, my second in command for political matters (prejudiced as I am against political officers), Arnold Chernyavsky, graduated from the
Moscow Political Academy and then tried to bring something new to the teaching of Marxism-Leninism at the naval
political academy in Kiev, for which he was summarily dismissed to the reserves.

On February 12, 1958, my former subordinates arranged a modest send-off for me. First I said goodbye to the enlisted seamen and petty officers. What wishes for me did they express upon parting? "Don't ever change." I was hardly a soft touch; if there was delinquency, I would sternly punish the culprits, although this rarely happened. I thanked all of them for this wish, thanked them for their service, and then in honor of the occasion we polished off a good dozen bottles of Massandra wine, not the dry stuff, but the real "Black Stone." (This was against regulations, of course, but I wasn't about to let that stop me. My superiors were aware that I was taking leave of my team.) Plus, my men had staged this send-off right in the barracks of the quadrangle where they lived; they weren't afraid. Then on February 12 I said goodbye to the career officers and petty officers. This was a warm send-off, during which they presented me a gift: a modest set of silver (three shot glasses and a little serving tray) and also a set of flatware (spoons, forks, knives) in cases inscribed *To our success and health. From the crew of Submarine S-98.* That silver set is my most prized possession, a souvenir of camaraderie and friendship.

But time was getting on. As for my superior officers, who had dumped on me royally on many occasions, I took my leave of them in strictly official fashion. I should point out that for them, my new commission was a complete surprise, particularly since in those days they didn't entrust just anyone with command of a nuclear vessel. So I took great pleasure in bidding those ignorant and ungrateful brigade commanders goodbye. I was never going to miss them. I had a future ahead of me now, a future I still had to discover and master. I believed in that future and devoted myself and my faithful family to it body and soul. I had no regrets at all. And just as before, the future would begin with hard work. And with the unknown.

★ ★ ★

ZATEYEV WOULD FACE formidable barriers, many of which were imposed by the vagaries of the new field of nuclear power. In all of his future challenges he would demonstrate his ability to focus on the primary mission of command, which was to create a combat-ready ship with an effective crew. Often throughout his ordeal he faced insurmountable problems caused by poorly constructed equipment and the absence of moral leadership qualities in his superiors. Yet his own competence, loyalty, and leaderhip abilities were never questioned.

=====

CHAPTER FOUR

THE SOVIET UNION was locked in a desperate race with the United States for supremacy in nuclear weapons: on land, in the air, and at sea. With an economy that was many times greater than that of the Soviet Union, the U.S. consistently pushed forward with new technology, escalating the arms race to ever greater heights. Throughout the Cold War the U.S.S.R. was forever playing catch-up. In its paranoid fervor for achieving parity with those who might attack the Soviet empire, grave errors were bound to occur. Captain Zateyev happened to be on the ground floor of many of the mistakes made with Soviet submarines.

The world's first nuclear-powered submarine, America's U.S.S. *Nautilus,* was powered by a single 70-megawatt thermal (MWt) pressurized water reactor delivering 15,000-shaft horsepower through two propellors. Later reactors would increase in power to as much as 220 megawatts thermal, delivering 60,000-shaft horsepower. As for range and endurance, the nuclear submarines were limited solely by the ability to support the crew with food.

America's first missile-firing nuclear submarine, the U.S.S. *George Washington*, launched its first Polaris ballistic missile in a test in July 1960. The Polaris missile had a range of 1,500 miles. It soon was replaced by the 2,800-mile-range Polaris A3 and Poseidon C3, and then the Trident C4 missiles, which extended the range to well over 3,800 miles.

The Soviet Union began its nuclear power program in 1956, moving quickly to the production of its first-generation submarines, categorized in the West by their propulsion systems, and termed the November, Echo, and Hotel classes. Each of these was fitted with two pressurized water reactors producing 70 megawatts and delivering 17,500-shaft horsepower in the November-class boats and 19,500-shaft horsepower in the other classes. The early Soviet marine reactor development program used nuclear-powered icebreakers as prototypes for the submarine reactors. By testing the reactors aboard surface ships the researchers hoped to gain more thorough and faster test results.

Soviet naval reactors used fuel in the form of uranium oxide containing Uranium 235, enriched to between 30 to 60 percent. The fuel was carefully machined into pins, which were then sealed inside cladding and arranged in bundles similar to those in land-based pressurized water reactors. Each reactor had eight bundles per core, divided into two distinctive halves of four zones. The 30 to 60 percent enrichment level used by the Soviets—which was lower than that used in most of the U.S Navy reactors, which are enriched typically to 97.5 percent uranium—necessitates a slightly larger diameter and deeper reactor pressure vessel, or casing, with a normal refueling interval of between two to four years. Most Soviet nuclear submarines were equipped with two reactors, both for reliability and for additional power.

The heat generated inside a nuclear reactor by uranium fission is transferred to a liquid coolant, called the primary coolant, which cools the reactor directly. This primary coolant may be liquid metal, or it may be very pure water. If the coolant is water, it must be kept under considerable pressure by the pressurizer system (hence the name pressurized-water reactor) so that it will not boil and interrupt heat flow from the reactor core. The primary coolant flows through tubes in a steam generator, where its heat is transferred to a secondary coolant, and then the colder primary coolant is pumped back through the reactor vessel to remove more heat from the reactor. The secondary coolant in the steam generator absorbs the heat from the primary coolant and boils, creating steam under pressure. It is this steam that drives both the main turbines, which in turn drive the two propulsion shaft or shafts; the steam also drives the electric turbogenerators. The steam from the turbine exhausts is then condensed by cool seawater flowing through tubes in condensers, and the condensate is pumped back into the steam via the propeller shafts— a system similar in most respects to a conventional steam-power plant on a surface ship. In addition to transferring heat to the secondary system, the continuous flow of primary coolant through an active reactor is critical for removing the heat and preventing damage to the core from overheating. Thus any interruption in the primary coolant flow can be fatal. In the first-generation Soviet submarines there were no backup primary cooling systems or emergency cooling systems. Because of this, the proper working of the pumps circulating the coolant was every bit as critical as the proper working of the reactor itself. One of the

worst possible failures a nuclear reactor can sustain is an interruption in the flow of or loss of primary coolant. In such an event
the reactor not only ceases to provide power, but also can be damaged by overheating and melting of the reactor's uranium fuel.
As a result of poor design and inept operation of the Soviet reactors, several cases of nuclear fuel meltdowns occurred, resulting
in large numbers of casualties and extensive radiation contamination. The most recent of these accidents was in the steam
explosion in Unit 4 in Chernobyl in April 1986. Details of all
these accidents were concealed by Soviet authorities.

The workings of a Soviet nuclear reactor are very well described
by Zateyev. In his later career he would become an expert on
nuclear safety in the fleet. His observations are a unique confirmation of what Western naval intelligence had long suspected:
The Soviet naval nuclear engineering plants and weapons systems were only marginally reliable.

★ ★ ★

A NUCLEAR REACTOR IS decidedly hazardous and has to be
safeguarded against accidents and disasters. Making a reactor secure from mishaps is no less complicated a task than
designing it in the first place. The likelihood of various categories of accidents is supposed to be taken into account during the development of *any* piece of new technology. To
preclude such accidents, reliable monitoring instruments plus
redundant automatic and manual safety mechanisms and
methods should be in place. The primary cooling loop of a
reactor consists of large-diameter high-pressure pipelines con-
necting the reactor to steam generators, pumps, and heat
exchangers, which are merely large condensers. This primary

loop also consists of compensation rods, which control the atomic fission process—which generates power to the main engines and other auxiliary assemblies. Because of the complexity of this primary circulation loop, it is difficult to design emergency procedures for repairing a leak in a seal or a rupture in one of the numerous pulse tubes, where the various monitoring gauges provide readouts on conditions inside the loops, which are in constant use. The worst possible reactor accidents are those involving a loss of liquid coolant during a sudden rupture in the primary loop pipeline. This is because the primary coolant is highly radioactive.

To contain a leak or rupture in this primary loop requires a series of key decisions to retain the integrity of the entire shielded zone of the reactor compartment. This shielded zone must remain intact for the entire duration of the accident to restrict the possible spread of nuclear fission by-products throughout the ship. This series of casualty-control measures must ensure sufficient heat removal to keep the nuclear fuel rods from melting. A cooled shield zone in the power plant itself must be maintained for the duration of the accident. This must be done by an emergency dousing or spray system, which directs jets of water into the reactor from special tanks using high-pressure pumps. Such casualty-control safety systems exist only in modern reactors. Our first-generation nuclear submarines had none.

The operating manuals of the time included strict instructions never to allow the reactor's sealed zone to become overheated under any circumstances; otherwise, a thermal explosion could occur. Exactly what a thermal explosion of such a reactor might entail was something we couldn't imagine and had never experienced. We knew nothing about the tank containing highly radioactive wastes at Kyshtym, which had exploded in Chelyabinsk in the Ural mountains on September 29, 1957, and officially, we still don't.

★ ★ ★

DETAILS OF THE CHELYABINSK accident are still guarded by the Government of the Russian Federation, although many facts about the terrible occurrence have leaked to the public. The exact numbers of those who died in the accident are still classified but are commonly suspected to be high.

At the beginning of his training, however, Zateyev didn't know anything about nuclear power. It was a brave new world he was entering, the great promise held out by nuclear fission. In these early days of his training, he began to focus all his powers on his new command, and like prospective commanding officers in every navy, he concentrated on selecting the best officers and key warrant and petty officers for his submarine.

★ ★ ★

WHAT SORT OF SHIP was this that I was going to command? It was the first Soviet nuclear-powered ballistic missile submarine. The chief designer of submarines of this project was Sergei Nikitovich Kovalyov, whom I knew from another prototype ship, the diesel-powered submarine S-61, for which he had been the deputy chief designer under Zosima Deribin and which had been built in the city of Nikoláyev (near Odessa in the Black Sea) in 1950-52. The keel for the K-19 was laid on October 17, 1958, at the N402 shipyard, now renamed the Northern Machine-Building Enterprise, in the city of

Severodvinsk (located in the White Sea near Archangelsk). The ship was launched on April 8, 1959.

The basic specifications and performance characteristics of the submarine are as follows:

- Surface displacement: 4,100 metric tons
- Submerged displacement: 5,600 tons (reserve buoyancy: 30%)
- Length: 114.1 m
- Armament (missile): 3 R-13 (SS-N-4) ballistic missiles (equipped with 1.4-megaton warheads)
- Armament (torpedo): 4 bow torpedo systems, 533 mm (total supply carried in tubes); 2 bow torpedo systems, 400 mm (total supply: 2 in tubes, 4 spare torpedoes on racks); 2 stern torpedo systems (total supply: 2 in tubes, 4 on racks)
- Surface speed: 15 knots
- Submerged speed: 26 knots

Its main armament was the ballistic missiles; eight torpedo tubes with spare torpedoes—the 533 mm torpedoes were nuclear-tipped—would make the submarine a formidable adversary for the antisubmarine forces of our likely enemy, i.e., NATO antisubmarine warfare forces, during a breakthrough or penetration of our antisubmarine defenses, and entry into our local operating areas. The range of the ballistic missiles was designed so that the ship could fire on NATO targets from the Atlantic from a distance outside the range of NATO's own local ASW forces. Its nuclear power plant gave the submarine a practically unlimited operating range and endurance—restricted only by the physical endurance of the crew, set by medical authorities at 60 days—and by its onboard food supply. What commander wouldn't be proud of a ship like that! As with anything new, one must know it well and learn how to use it. Before I could learn to command my new ship, I would have to undergo special training.

The Americans were already perfecting their first nuclear missile submarine, the *George Washington.* Meanwhile, under pressure from our country's political leadership, an accelerated nuclear submarine construction program was launched.

My arrival in Moscow fell on a pre-holiday period: The 40th anniversary of the Red Army was approaching. The deputy chief of the navy's submarine personnel department, Captain Third Rank Aleksandr Aleksandrovich Savelyev, invited me to stay with him for the holidays—he lived near Moscow's Kropotkinskaya metro station. I accepted, and then after the holiday, on February 24, I left for the training center. This center for military specialists had been set up in the first Soviet nuclear power plant in the city of Obninsk outside Moscow. Naturally, by the time nuclear submarine crews began training there, the center had a fully operational shipboard nuclear reactor on line. That reactor would be used to train us in servicing the power plant of a nuclear submarine. The subjects in the curriculum that were new to us were nuclear physics, reactor theory, basic quantum mechanics, dosimetry, the design of reactors and their control and safety systems, instrumentation, the design of the main turbine gear assembly, and the other systems and assemblies of the ship's steam power plant. I should note that the ship's operations department as well as the engineering department underwent special training at this center, while the remaining officers followed a standardized curriculum.

By the time I got to the Obninsk center, training was already in session. The officers considered the class much like academic education with a specialized curriculum. My first impressions of my officers were disheartening. For the most part, they were lieutenants who had graduated from the Dzerzhinsky Higher Engineering School in Leningrad and then immediately been assigned to the crew of the *K-19*. Before the start of training at the center, they had been temporarily posted to various ships—some in Kronstadt (the island base outside Leningrad), some in Leningrad, and some even in Tallinn and Liepaja (in the Soviet Republic of Estonia). In other words, they'd been shuffled around with nothing to do and no responsibilities. The crew's slovenliness and shirking were so extreme that, in literally a month's time, I was already forced to consider expelling a number of discipline cases from my crew. K. Klych, Kazakov, and three other incorrigible officers were in fact expelled. I would have to forge this group into a well-oiled and tightly knit crew.

The problem was further complicated by the fact that the training center was being run by a bunch of utter incompetents. The director was Captain First Rank Sokolov, who was drab, grossly overweight, and insolent. His deputy was Engineer Lieutenant First Class Yakubov, who was mediocre in his own right and no great shakes as an engineer, either. The training center staff were very smug about their positions and did exactly as they pleased. They actually built themselves *dachas* (cottages) using the labor of the crews being trained at the center, and they exploited our seamen and petty officers without consulting their commanders.

I should point out the apparent reason for this behavior on their part. Earlier, in 1954, the *K-5* crew had been trained originally as a reserve crew for the *K-3*, but later the navy decided not to have reserve crews. So the *K-3's* reserve crew became the crew of the *K-5*, the second nuclear submarine of the 627A project. Their initial training took place in Leningrad, and when they arrived at the nuclear power station in Obninsk, there was still no training center as such operating there, and they didn't acknowledge Sokolov's authority over them. True, they underwent practical training on the transport reactor, which was operating but not yet perfected structurally, under Sokolov and Yakubov; nevertheless they still remained aloof. So when the crews of Captains Second Rank Vasily Shumakov of the *K-8* and Boris Marik of the *K-14* arrived for training, these distinguished leaders of men apparently decided to show everyone what they were worth as commanders (here I'm talking about Sokolov and Yakubov, of course)—give a fool some authority, and God help you! Particularly since the commanders of these ships had been posted to their new jobs from ships that had been laid up for repairs. That meant that during their previous command of diesel submarines, they hadn't completed their qualifications to join the fleet of operationally ready ships, leaving them with a kind of inferiority complex. For that reason the two commanding officers allowed Sokolov and Yakubov to get away with bullying them, and put up no resistance to their tyrannizing and effrontery.

In my view, they lacked confidence in themselves as commanders. With me, the training officers had a much harder time of it. I wouldn't stand for any man raising his voice to me, and later when commanders like Valentin Rykov, Vladimir Chernavin, and Viktor Belashov—all from operationally experienced warships—showed up, Sokolov and Yakubov had to clean up their act. Soon, at the insistence of the commanding officers attending training, they were both dismissed from their posts and discharged from the service.

A few words about the training. Theoretically, the program was supposed to take nine months—based on eight hours of activities every day—and conclude in a series of exams on all topics. The theoretical course would be followed by practical training on the functioning reactor. This reactor was an experimental shipboard model belonging to the Ministry of Medium Machine Building, and the training center was simply "strapped on" to it, so that as the bugs were being worked out of the reactor systems, our submarine crews were simultaneously getting their reactor training. What this meant in practice is that we were always working around the designers' and builders' schedule of activating and deactivating the power plant. In other words, our practical training came second to their needs, which meant that the training took longer to complete. However, there was no need for my crew to hurry, because in early 1959 construction was temporarily suspended while the higher-ups made up their minds about which type of boats to build, ballistic-missile submarines or cruise-missile submarines. The period of indecision gave my crew a chance to complete the entire program of practical training on the operating reactor. All my officers were authorized by a commission made up of civilian specialists to operate a nuclear power plant independently.

So the training period was concluded—in my own view, quite successfully. I attended every qualification test and exam personally and learned exactly how well each of my subordinates knew his stuff. On March 7, 1959, the crew of the *K-19*, under the supervision of executive officer, Captain Third Rank Vladimir Velanov, departed for Severodvinsk. There the crew was joined by specialists of the other departments, and began learning the "iron." In other words, the men actually took part in the construction of the ship while, at the same time, learning their occupational specialties and the equipment. They also learned the organization of their duties according to the various ship's operating watch, quarter, and station bills (the master plan organizing the crew into duty sections for watch standing, and all other duties).

★ ★ ★

WELL INTO THE 1980s, Soviet submarine-launched ballistic missiles were boosted by liquid-fuel engines. Liquid missile fuel has certain advantages. It can be throttled, stopped, and restarted more easily than solid-fuel motors. Yet liquid-fueled missile engines are larger and more complex than solid-fueled, are much more unstable and volatile, and consequently extremely dangerous to transport. Liquid tanks and fuel lines must be inspected often to guard against moisture. The early Soviet liquid-fuel missiles were fueled shortly before launch. In the SS-N-6, which was the mainstay missile system from 1967 to 1986, liquid fuel was stored inside the missiles themselves in the tubes and had to be periodically replaced as a safeguard against tank corrosion and evaporation. The comparative weight and bulkiness of liquid-fuel missiles help explain why the long used SS-N-6 was 35 percent heavier and 50 percent taller than the American Polaris A-1 missile. The ingredients of the Soviet-made liquid fuel included nitrogen tetroxide and hydrazine, which explode when mixed and launch the missile from the tube. The U.S. solid-fuel missiles were ejected by high pressure air and then ignited in the air above water. Accidents with liquid-fueled missiles and torpedoes cost the

Soviet Navy dearly. In January 1962 a torpedo exploded aboard the diesel-powered submarine *B-37* in the port of Polyarny, obliterating it and sinking another diesel boat moored alongside. In October 1986 in the Atlantic, leaking missile fuel in a silo aboard the nuclear-powered *K-219* exploded, causing the loss of that ship along with four men, 44 nuclear warheads, and two reactors in 18,000 feet of water. More recently, unstable liquid torpedo fuel sank the submarine *Kursk* in August 2000 in the Barents Sea.

★ ★ ★

WE RETURNED TO SEVERODVINSK in mid-August and in mid-October sea trials began for our ship. Because of the adverse ice conditions in the White Sea and the difficulty of conducting sea trials in the Barents Sea while based in the Kolsky Bay region, the government decided that the *K-19* should winter in Severodvinsk until the ice cleared on the White Sea. Until this decision came down, we'd been preparing to relocate to Zapadnaya Litsa (a port on the Kola Peninsula). The *Kapitan Melekhov* had arrived from the port of Arkhangelsk to provide us icebreaker escort. The icebreaker's captain and I had worked out our procedures, devised the necessary signals, in addition to the traditional escort maneuver signals, and gone over all the other issues involved in the icebreaker escort plan. The captain had graciously shown me around his ship, which I liked very much, especially the comfortable accommodations for the seamen. However, to my great disappointment, the trip was called off. It was if my heart sensed that this was somehow a bad omen, and in fact, it was.

At the same time we were there, the shipyard was rushing to deliver structurally completed Project 627A (*Kit* type

November class) nuclear-powered attack submarines to the navy. There were three of them: *K-5, K-8,* and *K-14.* These ships were being completed in a hurry. The shipyard and government sea trial programs had been combined, telescoped, and abbreviated, taking no more than six or seven days at sea. Then without mechanical inspections, the ships were sent up north, with spaces and quarters unfinished and unpainted. Not one of these submarines was put through its complete program of trials. Their power plants and weapons systems were not comprehensively inspected, despite the fact that there was still a long way to go before the installation and testing of their reactors and reactor auxiliary systems would be completely finished. All three submarines left the shipyard with defects and incomplete assemblies and had to undergo repairs and final construction at their bases. During the summer of 1960 only one of them, the *K-14,* was able to put to sea. She was rushed out to take part in the naval exercise called "Meteor," so that our political leaders could be told that the billions of our people's rubles that had been spent on the building of nuclear submarines hadn't been wasted.

The lead attack submarine, the *K-3,* later renamed the *Leninsky Komsomol*, remained berthed at the shipyard for so-called "experimental operation"; to put it plainly, she was unseaworthy. (As for "experimental operation" of a vessel, to this day I don't understand that term; there's no such concept or no clear definition of it in our naval terminology.) There was a complete overhaul of her mechanisms, instruments, and systems. The turbines were taken apart and so on. This work was performed slowly and deliberately. Essentially, this submarine was serviced by a shipyard work team and representatives of the equipment suppliers. All her instruments and mechanisms were sealed, and military personnel were barred from servicing them or opening anything up. Shortly before our own ship was to undergo sea trials, the K-3 made her second sea voyage, a relatively lengthy one, around Novaya Zemlya to the Kara Sea and back again the same way. These voyages were undertaken for the sole purpose of proving that the power plant was functional, nothing more. I recognize the value of these trips and actually regret not taking part in them myself. But the fact remains that on these runs, all the ship's mechanisms were serviced by the shipyard personnel; our navy specialists were only observers attached to the team shipyard workers.

While the K-3 was moored in its "experimental operation" regime, the most incredible, laughable things happened. Some instrument or mechanism would stop working, and the operator would immediately call it a "breakdown"— they had no experience in the practical maintenance of these things—and then, panicked, put in a call for a specialist from the manufacturer. The specialist (in U.S. terminology, a manufacturer's technical representative) would quickly pack up his things and fly in from somewhere in the Urals or Siberia. Once he arrived, he'd look over the "broken-down" equipment, curse out the bosses who'd sent him, and replace some ordinary burnt-out fuse on the spot, then fly back to the Urals the very same day. These things happened plenty of times. This left the naval personnel with no chance to acquire skills in operating and maintaining their equipment. It was a long time before K-3 was finally qualified as operationally combat-ready.

To return now to my own ship, the K-19: Wintering in Severodvinsk was hard both on the crew and on the ship. During a test of the submarine's starboard reactor in April 1960, due to an error by the technical representative working on the control and protection system, a serious accident took place. A quench baffle got jammed in its lowered position, effectively disabling the reactor. The shipyard executives blamed my subordinates; the navy brass sided with the industry people.

I was on leave at the time of the accident, and by the time I returned and started objectively sorting out what had happened, with my whole crew still in a state of shock, it was already too late: The train, as they say, had left the station. The guilty parties, i.e., my engineering department officers, were punished; I was disciplined, too. Three years later, the real culprit, shipyard technical representative machine adjuster Korchagin, was condemned to seven years in prison for this episode.

During post-accident repairs the number one reactor's core was replaced. In the process, we carefully observed and took part in the reloading of the reactor fuel rods.

★ ★ ★

A UNIQUE CHARACTERISTIC OF Russian reactors is the incorporation of a movable stainless steel structure, called a quench baffle, inside the reactor pressure vessel, which is used for immediate shutdown. When the reactor is running normally, the lattice-like baffle is positioned in the top part of the pressure vessel, withdrawn from the active reactor core. The quench baffle is also used when refueling the reactor and has been the cause of several major accidents. These occurred aboard Soviet submarines when the reactor lid was being removed prior to or replaced following fueling. Before the start of the refueling, the quench baffle is raised from the normal position to the top of the core, thus quenching the fission process so the reactor cover can be raised and the control rod assemblies fully withdrawn. At this point crewmen insert a temporary refueling cover that protects all but one of the eight fuel modules. This one element is then removed by a fuel canister inserted into the reactor compartment. After all eight spent fuel modules have been removed, engineers inspect the vessel and then manually insert the new fuel modules. Once all these are in place, the temporary cover is removed and the reactor cover is hoisted back into position ready to lower. Until this is securely in place the enriched fuel assembly is totally dependent on the quench baffle to prevent a restart of the fission process. Should the baffle for some reason become dislodged or slide down into its normal position, fission will commence and might escalate into an explosion. Such accidents happened several times while Soviet submarines were refueling. The most serious of these occurred in Chazma Bay in 1985, resulting in a huge explosion and the loss of ten lives.

The accident took place on August 10, 1985, aboard an atomic cruise missile submarine moored in the Pacific port of Shkotovo-22, 30 miles north of Vladivostok, undergoing nuclear-core refueling. During the preparations a leak was discovered under the reactor's cover, a defect that normally required dry-docking to fix. To save time, however, the crew and yard workers attempted repairs while the submarine was still in the water. During the process of raising the reactor cover to remove the spent fuel, two neutron-absorbing rods were accidentally extracted, triggering an uncontrolled chain fission reaction. The one-ton reactor cover was blown more than 100 yards high, then fell back onto the submarine. Radioactive fuel and the remains of ten crew and yard workers were scattered throughout the bay. The blast ejected the nuclear fuel and quench baffle in a huge plume of contamination containing an estimated four cubic meters of highly radioactive material over an area as large as the Chernobyl tragedy that drifted six kilometers toward the city of Vladivostok. Shortly after the explosion, dock workers and navymen were ordered to mop up and conceal the accident. According to witnesses, once the blaze was extinguished the gates of the shipyard were closed and workers who had participated in the cleanup were directed to shave off their hair, surrender their clothes, and take repeated showers. The workers buried the fragmentary remains of the ten men along with other contaminated debris in specially prepared pits. The submarine was towed to a remote pier and abandoned, stripped of its reactors.

The complex technology and training required for nuclear energy work pointed out glaring deficiencies that would burden the Soviet submarine building program. Nuclear power was hailed as a savior, while the dangers of its deadly radiation were downplayed. When combined with the inherent dangers that any underwater vessel faces, the results were potentially calamitous. Yet the Soviet Union would keep charging forward, ignoring each warning signal that was raised. The long-established navy and shipbuilding hierarchies were confronting a new and still more powerful organization called the Ministry of Atomic Energy, which was dominated by eccentric physicists and intellectuals who were not easily cowed. They, not the sailors, would call the shots. The beacon of nuclear power would not be dimmed.

TRIALS

═══

CHAPTER FIVE

 NCE A SHIP HAS completed the complex period following construction called fitting out, the next step is a series of trials, which vary in complexity from dock trials, conducted in port alongside a pier, to those performed at sea. Every system from main propulsion, navigation, weapons, and emergency equipment is subject to detailed testing. While shipyard workers and personnel from the design and building organizations are usually aboard for the trials, most commanding officers use this period to begin training their crews in efficient functioning of the shipboard watch organization.

Executive officer Captain Lieutenant Vladimir Yenin came aboard the *K-19* during the pre-commissioning period as the mine and torpedo officer. One of the original crew, he became the *starpom*, second in command, shortly before the *K-19* sailed. He had initially opposed many of Zateyev's harsh methods of discipline, but he was loyal to the captain.

Chief engineer Captain Third Rank Anatoly Kozyrev, the hardworking head of the engineering division, replaced the first chief engineer, fired by Zateyev for incompetence while in the pre-trial fitting-out period. Main propulsion assistant Captain Lieutenant Yuri Povstyev was a 28-year-old deputy to the chief engineer in charge of the reactors and main steam engines. He was known as a dedicated and hardworking officer and would prove invaluable to the ship's survival. Compartment Six Commander Lieutenant Boris Korchilov was innovative and brave. Commander of a reserve crew Captain Second Rank Vladimir Pershin was an experienced commander of an early nuclear-powered submarine. He came aboard the *K-19* at the last minute before sailing as one of the submarine brigade commander's liaison officers to observe the exercise.

Sea trials are critical for ensuring the safe and efficient operations of all the ship's equipment, especially the main propulsion engineering plant, not only for itself but also for each subsequent ship of the type to be built. When the first in a class is tested, the trials are more rigorous and detailed in order to detect design flaws and to determine the need for modifications. A steam pipeline, for example, may have to be rerouted, which would call for a revised flow analysis.

Once the prototype of the class has completed testing, and the shipyard begins series production of that model, trials required by subsequent submarines of that class are streamlined. In the race to establish a significant submarine force, however, trials for follow-on Soviet ships of a specific class were so greatly abridged that the margin of safety for their individual crews was minimal.

In July 1960, *K-19* started its initial sea trials in the White Sea, sailing out of Severodvinsk with a full crew and a number of shipyard supervisors aboard. Trials usually lasted two to three days and extended over four months.

In one critical test that Zateyev writes about, new construction submarines are tested at depths near to their maximum safe limit to verify tightness of fittings. Soviet submarines were built with double-hull construction learned from the Germans, with the inner, or pressure, hull surrounded by an outer hull made of softer material. A series of structural stiffening rings surround the pressure hull, reinforcing it to withstand full submergence pressure. The space between the inner and outer hulls is used for main ballast tanks, fuel ballast tanks, and other tanks equalized with sea pressure, and the outer hull can be made of a weaker material. This differs from American submarine construction, which uses largely single-hull configuration. In a single-hulled submarine, the stiffening rings must be built inside the pressure hull. The main ballast tanks in American submarines are located at either end of the ship, and, in some classes are wrapped around a portion of the pressure hull, thus forming inner and outer hulls in that section. Both systems provide the same results but with trade-offs. For two submarines of similar displacement, double-hull construction offers the advantages of greater interior space and greater resistance to damage, but has the drawback of making the submarine physically larger, and thus incurring a penalty in drag, the resistance to the submarine's motion through the water. That means that more power will be required to achieve the same speed. Single-hull construction results in a smaller submarine for the same displacement, but limits interior space somewhat and exposes the pressure hull to damage in combat. As a result, American submarine builders have long been more effective at efficient utilization of the interior space. Russian submarines' hulls have more internal space and compensate for the increased drag by using two reactors.

Soviet builders and the pre-commissioning crew of the new construction submarines, as in Western navies, were also required to conduct complete engineering sea trials. The most demanding of these was the full-power run, during which the ship would be required to build up speed to maximum power and steam for a given period of time while all areas of the propulsion plant were carefully checked for leaks or malfunctions. In the case of nuclear-powered submarines, one of the main items of concern was the safe operation of the reactors and the ability of the plant to collect and reuse the critical supply of feed water from the steam driving the turbines. This water, distilled originally from seawater, had be chemically pure. The success or failure of the full-power trial often depended on the ability of the engineering plant to conserve this feed water. For Soviet submarines, as with Western boats of this vintage, the full-power run was a significant hurdle in the trials.

Studying material from salvaged portions of a Soviet submarine in the Pacific in 1974, Western naval intelligence determined that the internal hull structure of early submarines was crude and apparently hastily assembled. One important item accomplished in early submarine engineering trials was adjusting the overall balance or trim of the boat. The initial lead ballasting is based on complex weight and moment calculations performed while a ship is at dry dock and cannot be checked until the ship is actually at sea. It is not unusual for these calculations to be off somewhat, but that most likely was not the cause of some of *K-19's* odd behavior Zateyev experienced and recorded in his memoir, particularly the event when the submarine heeled sharply while surfacing.

★ ★ ★

WE WERE VERY SERIOUS about our preparations for sea trials. Despite the manufacturers' wishes to curtail the testing program, the navy brass, in the person of Rear Admiral Andrei Chabanenko, insisted on carrying out the complete prototype version of the shipyard and the government sea trials without omitting a single point. We were getting the benefit of the recent dismal experience with the abbreviated sea trials program for the four unfinished Project 627A submarines.

On July 11, 1960, the navy flag was raised on submarine *K-19*, and that night at high tide, the ship put out to sea for the first time for her shipyard sea trials. I can't say they went smoothly. For that matter, the following government acceptance sea trials, which have different standards, were also pretty rough. The trial programs for commencing serial production of an entire class of submarines were much less elaborate than the trial programs for prototype ships. It took over four months to run through both prototype trial programs. There were breakdowns, malfunctions, readjustments, structural alterations, and so on. We had to make three attempts to perform just one dive to maximum operating depth. I should say a few words about one of those dives, our second run. On it something happened that none of us had anticipated, which very nearly ended in disaster.

These particular tests focused on compression of the pressure hull and the operations of the ballast systems at various depths. The gaskets of the external hull apertures didn't leak, and the vacuum pumps performed perfectly. Then at a depth of 290 meters a report came in from Compartment Six, the reactor compartment: "Small leak in the after section of the removable plate of the pressure hull." (Removable plates, or hull access plates, are cut in the hull to allow for loading and unloading of bulky mechanisms in port, such as circulation pumps for the reactors' primary cooling loops.)

There were two men in Compartment Six at the time: Captain Second Rank Nikolai Segachev and a designer who was there to record measurements of hull compression and deformation of various elements of the compartment. Under normal conditions the reactor compartment is unmanned and entered only periodically for inspections.

I asked Segachev, "Can we descend farther?" He replied that the leak was insignificant and that we could continue with our dive. With me in the command post was the chief designer, the chairman of the acceptance commission (in Western terminology, the ship's superintendent). We slowly descended to our maximum operating depth of 300 meters. I slowed to a crawl and gave the order to begin inspecting the hull and taking readings. Suddenly, in the midst of calm came a panicked report: "Compartment Six is flooding!"

I stood at the intercom and instructed Compartment Six: "Report your situation, calmly and immediately!" But the compartment was silent.

I can't stand uncertainty. I had to do something. The situation was unclear and could well become critical if the compartment really was flooding with seawater while we were at maximum operating depth. Manning the diving planes was the submarine's planesman, warrant officer Kisenko, the ship's experienced boatswain. At the diving control station was chief hull technician Ivan Kulakov.

Instinctively, I issued the order: "Boatswain, surface!" and rang up "Turbines slow ahead!" on the engine order telegraph.

I started counting off the seconds. Our depth remained at 300 meters. My next order was, "Half ahead!"

The depth remained unchanged. The ship began dragging its stern. The seconds were racing past. Still no word from Compartment Six; all we could hear was the noise of inrushing seawater. What was happening there? My mind pictured a kaleidoscope of different scenes. If the compartment flooded, the ship would lose buoyancy. We had to do an emergency ascent. I gave the order: "Blow the 'midships!" (that is, blow the midship group of diving ballast tanks). I remembered that before diving I had left my commander's set of compressed air cylinders—my personal reserve—unconnected to the ship's system. Now, to help Kulakov, I connected them to the compressed air column. More seconds passed. The stern dragged lower, but there was still no change in our depth.

Then I gave my final order: "Blow all main ballast!" There was the roar of high-pressure air rushing into the tanks. The seconds turned to minutes, and finally the sub began rising. I watched our depth and speed. At about 100 meters, at a speed of 12 knots, she started listing to port. I cut in the turbines.

The ship ascended rapidly, listing more and more. As we breached the surface, we were listing at a catastrophic 60 degrees. At this point there wasn't a thing I could do. I'd already done all that could be done in a situation like this. After an instant the list began correcting, shifting quickly to starboard, maybe to 40 degrees. We rolled back and forth a few more cycles until finally she returned to an even keel. There was complete silence in the central command post. I looked around at the men there with me. Sergei Kovalyov was white as a sheet. The acceptance commission chairman,

Captain First Rank Mazin, was in shock, shaking. The others, too, were in pretty bad shape.

I gathered my wits, climbed up into the sail, undogged the upper hatch, and emerged onto the bridge, taking a signalman with me. About a cable's length away off our starboard bow was the submarine tender that was escorting us on our sea trial. I waited before sounding the all-clear—we had dived while we were in general quarters (action stations). I wanted to give the crew a chance to collect themselves after experiencing such an unusual ascent. I climbed down from the bridge and spent a couple minutes pacing back and forth on the stern after deck, calming myself down. Then I returned to the bridge and gave the order to secure from general quarters.

So what had happened in Compartment Six? There was, in fact, a serious leak. Have you ever seen what a stream of water under 30 atmospheres of pressure can do? Once a long time ago, when I was still in the Black Sea Fleet, at a depth of 20 meters, a packing gland blew on a depth-gauge pipeline under the bulkhead about a meter from where I was standing. I had the impression of a powerful gush of water coming from somewhere topside that turned into spray and rain, along with a kind of roar you'll hear nowhere else.

This time the gush had come at a depth of 300 meters, filling the compartment with spray almost instantly, making orientation difficult, of course, and also making it difficult to determine the nature of the "hull breach" —what submariners call the source through which seawater penetrates the boat. What's more, the overwhelming suddenness of the accident had caused both men in the compartment to lose their nerve. But what had happened was simple.

Shortly before we put to sea for our deep-water dive, one of the main primary loop circulating pumps had been replaced. The large dimensions of the pump made it necessary to open the removable hull access plate over Compartment Six. Standard procedures call for replacing the special rubber gasket around the plate coaming; the plate itself is bolted to the coaming on the pressure hull. This time, however, the workmen who were removing the plate decided they'd save themselves a trip to the warehouse to get a new gasket by just reinstalling the old one, which they had to know was no longer serviceable. They installed it, screwed down the nuts, compressed it with as much effort as they deemed necessary, and reported to the acceptance engineer that everything was fine. The acceptance engineer reported the same to the ship's superintendent, who then reported to me that the pressure hull was fit for diving. Then, as we dived, the crushing pressure of the sea crimped in the deformed "old" gasket to a depth of 20 to 25 cm. along the perimeter of the plate. That's all it took: a very simple recipe for a hull breach.

The crew of our submarine tender was watching as we surfaced. Captain Second Rank Viktor Yushkov, standing on the bridge of that ship, later told me that the first thing they'd seen was a huge billow of water rising from the sea, followed by our submarine, literally lying on her port side as the hull heaved almost entirely out of the water and crashed back down, then rocked awhile from side to side before finally righting.

Thirty years later, at a celebration of the 30th anniversary of the raising of the flag on the *K-19*, the chief designer of our strategic nuclear submarines, Sergei Kovalyov, who had been aboard during that episode, told me that during the emergency ascent we had all been a hair's breadth away from death, and that we'd survived only by a miracle. As for me, I still remember that it took Kovalyov a good three hours after that surfacing to recover the gift of speech, while the ship's superintendent couldn't get out a single word until he'd set foot on shore again. That was one episode from our sea trials.

There were also instances of lack of discipline on the part of my crew. Luckily, these took place during steaming on the surface. The commander of the Third Division, the Damage Control Division of the Engineering Department, Engineer Captain Lieutenant Ye. P. Balabanov, actually tried throwing empty food crates away through the DUK, a device in Compartment Eight used to jettison containers of waste while underwater. (The DUK is a small air-lock chamber that uses a high-pressure piston to jettison containers filled with various everyday trash and garbage.) During this procedure, a board from a crate got stuck in the DUK. So Balabanov decided to open the front and back covers of the DUK and shove the board out of the ship by hand. It was a good thing we were on the surface, because as soon as the back cover of the container was opened, water came gushing in and was soon flooding the compartment. When the men realized what was happening, they sealed off the compartment and created a counter-pressure by bleeding in high-pressure air. The toll from Balabanov's absolutely oblivious actions was several electric motors flooded by salty seawater, including the main dehumidifier and air conditioner. How was I supposed to react to this? The culprit couldn't possibly remain on my ship. Although it cost me great effort—Balabanov was the son of some government minister—I did manage to rid myself of this so-called chief damage-control officer.

One particularly hazardous trial was the testing of the main power plant at our full speed of 26 knots running non-stop for 24 hours with both reactors operating at 100 percent of capacity, followed by a two-hour run at 110 percent. These trials took place in a restricted operating area of Kandalaksha Gulf at a depth of 60 meters. What made these trials so hazardous was that the sea is always the sea, even if we happened to be in an inland body of water in our own country. The effects of this full-power run still had not been extensively studied, since until we were tested there had been no need for such extensive study. And yet what could happen during more than 26 hours of submerged steaming at full power? How might the ship's position be affected by currents and other factors?

Sailing directions for the White Sea show that the bottom behaves in a very curious way under the influence of both continuous and tidal undersea currents. Little hills of sand that we call "cats" seem to "crawl" around the bottom, changing their location and height. As was shown years later, a good number of submarines made contact with these "cats" during sea trials. One submarine, which was carrying an acceptance commission chairman, Vice Admiral A. I. Sorokin, and the former navigator for a flotilla of nuclear submarines, Captain First Rank Lev Antokin, actually plowed into an underwater cliff at 24 knots. The cliff was marked on the charts, but the captain had simply failed to reckon with prevailing conditions and had violated training range rules. The ship survived only by a miracle. The outer hull on the starboard side was completely demolished all the way to the compensation tank (three-quarters back along the length of the hull) along with the attached

hydrophones of the sonar station. If the sub had been heading a fraction of a degree to starboard—a difference of only
two meters—she would have collided head-on, and there
would have been no survivors.

★ ★ ★

A KEY FACTOR THAT differentiated American from Soviet
nuclear-powered submarines of the early era was the external
noise produced by their power plants. When it was discovered
that the U.S.S. *Nautilus* was as loud as a freight train, sound
suppression in American submarines grew by leaps and bounds
until they were far quieter than their Soviet counterparts. The
first-generation Soviet submarines were notoriously loud. This
wide gap in stealth persisted for many years until American
secrets were betrayed by John Walker, Ronald Pelton, and
Aldrich Ames. In addition, some allied countries violated the
restrictions placed on export of sensitive engineering tech-
nologies, and Soviet designers were able to vastly improve their
quieting. The second-generation submarines, referred to as the
Charlie, Victor, and Yankee classes, launched in 1962 and 1963,
were still noisy. Only with their third-generation nuclear submarines, which appeared in the early 1980s, did the Soviet
power plants begin to challenge American submarines in
stealth. Until the late 1980s, the U.S. Navy was able to base
its entire antisubmarine warfare superiority on the ability to
fingerprint each Soviet submarine, not only by class but also
by individual boat, and to create an acoustic database that was
extremely accurate. As Captain Zateyev indicates, all Soviet
submarine commanders of that early era were acutely aware of
their vulnerability.

★ ★ ★

THE SIGNING OF THE submarine acceptance certificate still lay ahead. Here I must back up a little in my description of these events. One of the major factors involved in testing a submarine is its sound quieting, which allows it to operate undetected. I was aware that all four of the torpedo attack (multipurpose) submarines commissioned by the navy did not possess this quietness. Nor was the *K-19* any better than any of them in that respect. During her sea trials we spent a number of days measuring the noise of her auxiliary mechanisms; we tested them both under way and dead in the water. When I was handed the form listing the noise figures, I literally clutched my head in despair. The decibel numbers set down there in black and white were simply stunning. My experience at sea as a diesel submarine commander told me that unless I did something about this, I was going to be morally responsible for accepting a ship for our navy that was unfit for combat. I decided not to sign the acceptance certificate and instead raised the issue with the government. I gave the shipyard director advance notice of my decision. That was what started all the trouble. On two occasions shipyard director Yevgeny Yegorov summoned me so that he could pressure me to quit balking and sign the acceptance certificate. The second meeting ended in a stream of threats and obscenities: "I'm going to call the commander in chief this minute, and tomorrow you're not going to *be* a commander any more, you mother-friggin' idiot," and so on. I gave him back as good as I got, told him to go to hell, and walked out of his office. The next day I was summoned to Northern Fleet Headquarters and told that Fleet Commander Admiral Andrei Chabanenko had asked me to call him. I spoke with him directly. Chabanenko told me he'd been called by the Commander in Chief of the Navy, Fleet Admiral S. Gorshkov, who had ordered him to commission the submarine K-19 into the navy regardless. The fleet commander advised me to stop resisting and to give up the fight. After that, what was there left for me to do?

On November 12, 1960, the acceptance certificate was signed for the prototype nuclear-powered strategic ballistic missile submarine K-19. The signing ceremony was followed by a banquet at the shipyard entertaining facility called Engineers' House. At a certain point during the banquet the shipyard director, Yegorov, invited the top commanders present to adjourn to the closed room of the restaurant we called Edelman's Place, where the celebrations continued. There were, thank God, no incidents and no reprimands.

Captain First Rank Anatoly Sorokin, the commander of our nuclear submarine brigade, arrived from Zapadnaya Litsa to oversee preparations for our relocation to the K-19's permanent base. On November 16 we left for the north, arriving at Zapadnaya Litsa on the 18th. The next day we settled into accommodations aboard the tender for atomic submarines *Magomed Gadzhiyev*, commanded by Captain Second Rank Molochko. Routine combat training commenced. Or more accurately, our submarine joined in the effort of preparing for operations.

Zapadnaya Litsa Bay is best described as a fjord off the Barents Sea at the western extreme of the Kola Peninsula, close to Norway, with a narrow inlet leading to a bay divided into three smaller inlets: Malaya Lopatka, Bolshaya Lopatka, and Nerpichya. The bay is accessible by three routes: by sea from

Motovsky Bay, by land via dirt road from Ura Harbor—27 kilometers distant—or by another dirt road from Ura Harbor via the Pechenga route—also 27 km. In those early years the American press ran stories about the new Soviet naval base at Zapadnaya Litsa that were filled with amazement at how the Russians were basing their nuclear submarines in a region that was inaccessible by either paved highways or railroad, and supplying such base facilities by sea transport, which was very difficult and expensive. That was how our potential adversary regarded our buildup of the new base. Construction of its infrastructure was still only in the planning stage, and in our view, we were going about things the right way. Take the following episode, for instance, from the construction efforts of those years.

Sometime in mid to late January of 1961 we finished with the first phase of our ship's combat training program. A violent storm had been blowing for several days, with blizzard conditions and freezing temperatures. The lakes in the highlands from which we drew our freshwater supply for the support ships and coastal units had all frozen over. The water barge that brought us water from Severomorsk had been restricted to base by fleet headquarters—the wind was reaching hurricane force. The road to Ura Harbor was so snowed over that no vehicle of any type was ever going to make it out to us. The storm had already lasted two days, there was no letup on the third, and no telling when there would be any break in the weather. The brigade commander summoned me to see him aboard the support vessel *Dvina* and asked me whether my ship was ready to hand in its first assignment report. Preparations for this assignment culminated in the start-up of the ship's main power plant, i.e., her reactors. I answered that the ship was ready; all that remained was to start up the reactors. He replied with an order that was also a kind of request: All right, power them up, then get cracking on your first "combat" mission. You're going to "boil" enough water to supply all of us, because at this point the whole brigade, all the support ships and all the coastal units, have run out of fresh water. We were about ready to start melting snow! Since the *K-19* had two evaporators (for distilling fresh water from seawater), their output could easily supply the whole base with fresh water. I was pleased: This meant we would ace the final item of the test.

I replied, "Aye aye, sir!" and set about my task. That's what the process of "breaking in" the new base facility was like for us.

In February we handed in our first readiness report to the Severomorsk Northern Fleet Submarine Force Headquarters. We had prepared for it very thoroughly. The entire submarine force headquarters under Rear Admiral Aleksandr Petelin grilled every last one of us on everything with exaggerated diligence, i.e., needling us, determined to find fault wherever possible, then accepted our readiness report with a grade of "good."

Our second readiness assignment consisted of making preparations for a month-long patrol during which we would cover all aspects of controlling the submarine on the surface and submerged, in emergencies and other contingencies. Correcting significant defects that turned up in the work done at the shipyard took much of our time.

On April 2, the submarine *K-19* put to sea to perform her second readiness assignment. We had an interesting experience upon first entering the combat training range, which for us was going to be above the 71st parallel in the Barents Sea. We took the recommended channels to get there. After leaving Motovsky Bay, we headed directly east, and once we had

Teriberka off our starboard quarter, we headed due north for the 71st parallel and our training range. Before setting our course northward, I decided to climb to periscope depth and get a radar fix on our exact position before leaving radar range of the coast. We ascended to periscope depth, fixed our position with respect to the coastline, then turned north.

The sonarmen reported noise off our port side. I scanned the horizon through the periscope: nothing seen visually. There was nothing on any of the radar scales, either, except the contour of the coastline at the extreme range of our radar. I concluded that there was no one out here but ourselves. However, the noises continued coming in loud and clear. We submerged and continued on our course. I ordered the watch officer to perform a baffle-clearing maneuver every two hours in order to listen in on our stern sector. Each time we zigged or zagged, we heard that same noise: the screws of an unidentified vessel doggedly following in our baffles. I analyzed the situation and concluded that we'd picked up an American submarine. In fact, this wasn't the first indication we'd had that the Americans were entering our waters and conducting surveillance of our nuclear submarines.

Once we had taken up our position in the training range, we began running through the various phases of our assignment. Everything proceeded smoothly until April 12. That day would be a turning point.

At 4:00 a.m., just after a change of watch, the watch officer was Captain Lieutenant Mukhin (that is, the officer who stands duty on the bridge while the ship is under way); the watch engineer was Captain Lieutenant Povstyev. Depth: 60 meters; speed: 16 knots; heading: 270 degrees; conditions normal. I left the Central Command Post for my cabin in

Compartment Two. After no more than five minutes I sensed the ship starting to pitch down by the bow. Usually a pitch of two or three degrees doesn't bother me. This time, however, she dropped lower than that. I immediately ran back to the CCP. Quick reactions to changes in pitch and list were by then a matter of instinct for me. The second anything happened, I would run for the CCP. No emergency drills had been included in the plan for this assignment. We'd already finished every phase of the exercise, and in a couple of days we were planning to return to base to load practice torpedoes and missiles for our third and fourth assignments. When I entered the CCP, my first impression was that the watch did not have the situation in hand. No measures were being taken, while our downward pitch grew more severe with every second. I grabbed the engine order telegraphs and signaled orders for full reverse thrust by both turbines. Next I gave Diving Control the order, "Bubble bow buoyancy!" and followed that immediately with, "Blow the midships group!" I glanced at the depth gauge—260 meters—then ordered, "Blow all main ballast!" I was issuing orders in rapid-fire succession, but they were carried out precisely and immediately. I was a little late with the command "Both turbines, full speed ahead!" when our pitch began reversing. We switched the turbines to forward thrust when our pitch was back to 10 or 12 degrees, but that was no problem: The ship was ascending.

So what had happened? It was very simple, really. A young seaman—we'd taken ten young seamen trainees with us on this operation—had decided to clean the power supply board for the stern diving plane servomotor, and not knowing any better, he'd yanked out a fuse in the plane motor circuit. Under their own weight, the planes had dropped to their full "dive" position. We were using the smaller stern planes at the time, and that could have been what saved us. We surfaced more or less without incident. I didn't even have time to sound an emergency alarm or general quarters; that's how fast everything happened. I sounded general quarters only after I'd dogged open the hatch to the conning bridge.

On the surface it was night, zero visibility, not a star in the sky. I took a step onto the bridge and felt my foot sink into something sticky. The navigator handed me up a flashlight; I switched it on and was instantly horrified. I was standing almost up to my knees in liquid, gray sea silt. The whole bridge was completely covered in it. A report came from the CCP that the stern planes were in complete working order. There was a storm blowing on the surface, waves two or three meters high, wind out of the north, banks of blinding dense snow fog. I asked how much of our air we had left, and the answer was about 50 percent. I decided to dive to periscope depth to wash the silt off the bridge and superstructure. Meanwhile, I was trying to figure out how we could have gotten silt on the bridge. Even if we'd bottomed out, we couldn't possibly have sunk up to the bridge; or had we? I surmised that we'd only "kissed" the bottom, and that the screws had thrown silt over the bridge as our inclination tilted back to the stern while our engines were still in reverse.

We descended to periscope depth for ten minutes and let the seawater passing over our hull scour the superstructures and bridge clean. Then we surfaced again and began recharging our pressurized air with the two diesel compressors. I ordered a stand down from general quarters. I decided that we would remain on the surface until our pressurized air was completely replenished. Then we would dive again and resume work on certain phases of our assignment. However, there was no avoiding a critique of the watch officer's actions during the loss of trim we'd just experienced.

After breakfast at 8:00 a.m. I ordered that all watch officers assemble in the wardroom. The boat was running on her electric motors, making about six knots. The radar indicated several surface targets, small fishing vessels; the sonar operators regularly got a sound bearing on the noise of their propellers, and since they were a good long distance away, we could safely concentrate on our critique of what had just happened. I turned the bridge over to my second in command for political affairs, Captain Third Rank A. I. Shipov. I was planning to critique the actions of each man individually in as much detail as possible, turning the incident into an object lesson for the future, going over the steps to take in such situations.

The bulkhead hatch leading to the CCP from Compartment Two (where the wardroom was located) was left undogged in case I was called to the bridge. The clock read 9:11a.m. when suddenly I heard a command from the bridge: "Both engines, full reverse! General quarters alert!" I rushed into the CCP and onto the conning bridge. From there I saw directly ahead of our stempost the black mast of a periscope approaching from our starboard side, leaving a white feather wake, the glass eye of its lens turned in our direction.

We avoided a collision by about three meters. Luckily, our speed was low, and the engines were able to retard the ship's momentum. I asked Shipov when he'd detected the periscope. He reported that when he took over the conn from me, all targets on the radar screens were far off, and sonar was also tracking them. Shortly before the alarm was sounded, a sonar operator had suddenly reported that the noise from one object on our starboard had become much louder. The target was clearly approaching us, and very quickly. A radar scan on that bearing showed only a barely visible target at a great distance. Shipov peered into the bank of snow fog off the starboard bow, but visibility was almost zero. The radar operator detected no close-in targets. The snow fog passed over to our port side, and that was when the flagman and watch officer caught sight of a black log-like object bearing down on us fast—the periscope. Shipov's reaction had been correct. He had to avoid a ramming collision, so he ordered both engines back full and sounded general quarters.

If I hadn't seen that periscope with my own eyes, I'd never have believed his story. According to current fleet regulations, I was obliged to immediately report this encounter with an unidentified submarine. As I was writing out my message, the cryptographer—Petty Officer 1st Class Troitsky—handed me a radio message with the following message: "TO THE COMMANDER: REMAIN ON THE SURFACE. —FLEET COMMANDER." Fifteen or 20 minutes later, we heard a radio report: "A man has reached outer space... ."

Meanwhile, at my instructions the sonar operators continued tracking the unidentified submarine. She was heading north for the edge of the ice at high speed. We tracked her for about an hour until at 10 a.m. we lost the noise of her propellers.

Two days later, I was summoned to Severomorsk by the Northern Fleet commander, who interrogated me in great detail about our encounter with the foreign submarine. I learned that the moment he'd received my contact report, he'd informed the commander in chief of the Navy, Fleet Admiral Gorshkov. The fleet admiral had listened carefully to his information, then said that intelligence reported that the U.S.S. *Nautilus* was operating in this area of the Barents Sea. He was unhappy with me, as the commander of the *K-19*, for failing to ram it when I had the chance. "For *that*, we'd certainly have come up with the money to repair the stempost."

I said that I wouldn't have behaved at sea like a pirate, even if someone ordered me to ram the ship. Admiral Chabanenko sided with me. I took offense at being rebuked for not sinking the *Nautilus*. I wonder if her captain knew that night that he could have been looking at the world above the sea for the very last time. I knew that the *K-19's* stempost was made of specially hardened steel and would have survived a ramming impact, but the *Nautilus's* pressure hull would almost certainly not have.

★ ★ ★

ZATEYEV'S ACCOUNT OF the *K-19's* confrontation with the U.S.S. *Nautilus* has been verified by U.S. Navy records. Most of the incidents of alleged collisions and near collisions made by Soviet submarine commanders, however, have not been acknowledged by the U.S. Navy. More than 30 years after these events, the Navy refuses to discuss submarine operations, especially those of U.S. submarine reconnaissance operations conducted near the periphery of the Soviet Union. Throughout this history and most other accounts of the Cold War naval confrontation, accusations by the Soviets and Russians of collisions with Western submarines appear frequently. The Soviet Navy has, at one time or another, publicly alleged that losses of three of their submarines were caused by collisions: *K-129* in the Pacific in March 1968; *K-219* in the North Atlantic in October 1986; and *K-141*, the *Kursk,* on August 12,

2000. These claims were made immediately following each loss, and they have never been recanted by senior officers of the Russian Navy, except in the recent case of the *Kursk*. Russian investigators admitted in February 2002 that the *Kursk* did not collide with another ship.

Many submarine collisions did occur throughout the Cold War— according to the U.S. Navy, more than 25. Senior Russian admirals frequently complained to U.S. authorities about the behavior of American submarine commanders, especially those captains of U.S. attack submarines. On many occasions during the annual reviews of the agreement to avoid dangerous incidents at sea, in effect since 1972, Russian admirals complained pointedly that American submarine commanders frequently acted carelessly and drove their submarines such as to cause danger of collision. The factor that probably played the most decisive role in these close encounters was the long superiority in stealth of U.S. submarines and the greater operational autonomy American submarine commanders enjoyed. Although at times the behavior of these commanders might appropriately be characterized as reckless, American commanders were head and shoulders better trained and more adept than their Russian counterparts, who suffered immensely from relative inexperience and the heavy hand of the ever present political officer.

★ ★ ★

WE REMAINED ON THE surface, replenishing our air supply and charging the batteries. Soon after we transmitted our radio report about encountering another submarine, we received orders to take up a new position in a region to the northwest, beyond the 73rd parallel. While steaming for our new location, we finished charging our air tanks and batteries. Just before arriving at our new coordinates, we submerged and began methodically reviewing the day's events.

The next day we received orders to relocate to a combat training range for torpedo-firing exercises, which would be commanded by Admiral A. Sorokin on a destroyer. The goal of these exercises was for nuclear-powered ballistic missile submarines to fire a minimum number of torpedoes at both a single target ship and also an ASW ship engaged in a counterattack. The executive officer would carry out the firing of an additional torpedo. We ran through all three shots in a single day. This was my first experience of the "Leningrad" TAS (torpedo-firing computer) in action. It's a good device, but without additional complex maneuvering—which during a rapidly unfolding attack can be impossible to execute in time—it may be impossible to define the elements of the target's motions such as target angle. In such situations you would have to use either the periscope or radar, if only during the first phase of the attack, at least to get a single range to target, and then execute the rest of your maneuvers by sonar, judging the target's speed characteristics based on its variation of propeller revolutions. In reality, however, what attack submarine is going to take the risk of coming to periscope depth and using its active radar, too?

We had one bitter disappointment. When the executive officer fired his shot, the torpedo was lost. A large wave came up, and the torpedo essentially vanished from sight. A month later it was found smashed to bits on the rocks of Rybachy Peninsula, which at least absolved us of the sin of possibly having sunk the torpedo upon firing.

After the torpedo shoot, we had a missile-launching exercise. The scenario called for launching a missile from Mezen Bay after breaking through a line of ASW defenses. That was the end of our combat training at sea and the end of the overall combat-training program for our ballistic missile submarine. On April 29, 1961, we returned to base.

The next day, that is, on April 30, 1961, by order of the fleet commander, the submarine *K-19* was commissioned as an operational naval combatant and pronounced fully combat-ready. Rear Admiral Andrei Chabanenko congratulated me on my successful completion of combat training and added that he wanted the submarine ready to take part in the navy's June exercises.

Ashore, it was business as usual, of course. The minute you return from patrol, you're told to prepare to put to sea again. Our May Day celebrations were modest, because most of our team was busy with the ship's power plant, maintaining and cooling the reactors. The Mine and Torpedo Department officers readied a combat supply of torpedoes for loading; the missile officers readied the launch system to accept missiles. The Operations and Navigation Department officers prepared for the coming patrol to the Atlantic. There wasn't a minute left over to relax, but every last member of the crew was excited. We were about to take a Soviet nuclear missile submarine out for her first patrol on the open seas.

While the sub was berthed at Zapadnaya Litsa, during preparations for a patrol designed around combat-training assignment No. 2, a seal failure in the cover of the number two reactor—later traced to the "purge valve"—gave the engineering department a rich opportunity for hands-on training in the servicing of every segment of the power plant without help or guidance from either the manufacturer or the navy. For almost two months they regularly scrammed, cooled down, and then started up again reactors that had lifted safeties and vented pressure to atmosphere. (This occurs when the reactor heats beyond a safety point and is vented to prevent an explosion.) I must stress that we never got help from a single soul outside the crew during all the manipulations and testing needed to correct the unintentional venting aboard our ship. The commander of the Engineering Department, Captain Third Rank Anatoly Kozyrev, and the commander of the Propulsion Division, Captain Lieutenant Engineer Yury Povstyev, spent every hour of every day aboard that ship. The reactor control and instrumentation specialists left the ship only when it was a matter of practical necessity. The training missions at sea that followed—which were carried out in strict accordance with the full program of the Combat Training Course in terms of days under way and the elements of each assignment—gave still more experience to the entire engineering department.

Meanwhile, the construction of our nuclear submarines had become the focus of intense euphoria. This reached a kind of peak following the first brief cruise of the *K-3* in the Kara Sea in 1960 and the *K-14's* performance in the December 1960 *Meteor* exercises, which was represented as vindicating the great hopes placed in our nuclear submarines' combat capabilities. Putting a stop to all this was already out of the question. The rational criticism and proposals of the wiser heads in the leadership were going unheeded; these people were ignored and soon came to be persecuted. Propaganda kept harping on the imperialist threat, dinning into everyone's head that the "capitalist encirclement" was preparing to wage war on us and that the Soviet people must be well prepared to meet the enemy's treachery in a state of heightened military readiness. The politicians and military-industrial leaders played on the patriotic feelings of our people, who believed the propaganda and responded to these displays of "concern" for them by declaring, "We'll give up everything for the sake of avoiding a war." This tactic won these politicians and industrialists all the material perks they could wish for, and, most important, it freed them of any accountability for their actions— including the building of a fleet that was not combat worthy. Our leaders at every level crowed to the country and the world about what a mighty power we were, what sophisticated technology and what superior weapons systems we possessed. Against the backdrop of this euphoria, medals, stars, and prizes of all sorts were awarded indiscriminately, as were promotions and so on and so forth. Meanwhile, the fact that our ships were languishing at their piers at Zapadnaya Litsa because of technical malfunctions or for lack of armaments somehow didn't seem to register on anyone. To be fair, there were some modest attempts by the navy to rein in this bacchanalia.

In March 1961, the submarine tender *Dvina,* commanded by Captain Third Rank Mrktychan, hosted a conference of navy brass and leaders of the shipbuilding industry. On the table was the question of the reliability of our shipboard nuclear power plants, their major components and auxiliary equipment: the main and auxiliary circulating pumps of the primary cooling loop, the steam generators, pipelines, and electric pump armature of the fourth cooling loop, and so on. Why had this issue come up?

In practice, nearly every time one of our submarines put to sea, some segment or other of its power plant would malfunction. As a rule, it was an auxiliary circulating pump, or a leak in a steam generator causing a release of radioactivity, or a leak in the fourth cooling loop. Once the earliest atomic submarines, the K-5, the K-8, and the K-14, had arrived for permanent basing at Zapadnaya Litsa, our fleet commander, Admiral Chabanenko, raised the issue of the reliability of their power plants. The malfunctions effectively rendered the ships inoperable. The shipyards blamed the navy, claiming everything was due to the ignorance and incompetence of the crews, while the sailors blamed the shipyards for supplying the navy with unserviceable equipment. There was, of course, an element of truth to the claims of both sides. The fleet commander declared officially that the current practice of delivering defective equipment to the navy was absolutely unacceptable. Newly constructed ships had to be delivered in combat-worthy condition rather than laying them up for repairs immediately upon acceptance from the shipyard, as was the case with K-3, K-5, and K-8. For that matter, the K-14 was in service for only a year before it, too, had to put in for running repairs.

On the other side, the deputy minister of shipbuilding, Yury Derevyanko, furiously heaped the blame on the navy. The conference finally adopted a compromise decision that was supposed to settle the question of which side was right. Representatives of both the navy and the shipyards would take one of the most recently commissioned nuclear submarines, i.e., the K-19, the K-33, or the K-55, for a so-called "test run" that would demonstrate the reliability or the unreliability of the equipment and the crew's ability to service the power plant. Because of the repairs being made to the failed seal in the lid of the K-19's number two reactor, our ship was not chosen to be tested by the high-ranking commission. During one meeting I lost my temper and referred sarcastically to those present as the "saviors of the Great Russian Navy," which got me into deep trouble with Derevyanko and the navy's deputy director of combat training, Rear Admiral V. M. Prokofyev.

The submarine taken out for the "test run" was the *K-33*, commanded by Captain Second Rank Viktor Yushkov. After 48 hours at sea, the submarine came limping back from the area of Medvezhy Island on its diesel generators, the industry leaders aboard her disgraced. But even so, the only conclusion drawn from this failed attempt to besmirch the navy was that the ships already in large series production should continue being built. Working the kinks out of the technical systems and assemblies would be put off until the future. This might have made sense if only the power plant were involved. But there were deficiencies in the sonar and communications systems, and worst of all, the ships were noisy.

Getting ahead of myself somewhat, I should note that in October 1961, at a high-level conference at Navy Headquarters in Moscow, I let loose and declared unflinchingly that operating vessels that had to return from the sea because of technical malfunctions was positively shameful. Even before then I had argued quite vocally that we should first build one or two experimental subs, perfect all their systems and equipment to the point that we could guarantee their reliability, and only then launch serial production. But nothing doing. We continued building ships that were not combat worthy. As for me, I paid a high price, of course, for being so outspoken at meetings, conferences, and in various inner circles. At this particular conference I was supported only by Admiral Chabanenko (he and I were the only fleet representatives present). We were both immediately dubbed "men of little faith" by the first deputy commander in chief of the Navy, Admiral Kasatonov, who was chairing the meeting. This continued to be one of Kasatonov's favorite labels for people when he was appointed commander of the Northern Fleet, which happened soon after, in February 1962. Vice Admiral Anatoly Sorokin was especially fond of quoting back to me what I'd said at that meeting—that ships that were not combat ready were built by people who knew for certain that war was not a possibility and were hoodwinking the public, earning themselves rewards, privileges, and unmerited recognition.

The showers of military decorations continued. Hundreds of medals were given out; "Heroes of the Soviet Union" appeared by the dozens. And the shameless and brazen campaign to smear the people who actually cared about the interests of the navy also continued. The Northern Fleet commander, Admiral Chabanenko, was dismissed from his post, and shortly afterward his supporters and sympathizers were removed from leadership positions. The path of least resistance was to support an unscrupulous shipbuilding industry and those in the navy command who sided with it. That was how we ended up building a fleet of nuclear submarines that were not combat ready. The entire first generation of our nuclear subs and the greater part of the second generation were doomed to be destroyed in the very first days or even hours of a war. For that matter, the third generation of ships, today's generation, doesn't have much to recommend it over the first.

Perhaps our country's top leadership did not know, and did not want to know, that we were building ships that would be of no use in a war. After all, the leadership's general incompetence made them easy enough to fool. One instance was the famous incident at a "showcase demonstration" of a cruise missile that the Pacific Fleet staged for the top leadership, including Khrushchev. When the missile dropped into the sea seconds after liftoff (its starter engines had failed), our commander in chief, Admiral Gorshkov, assured Nikita Sergeyevich (Khrushchev) that it was now continuing on its course *underwater*. At that, our head of state declared in a booming voice to all present: "These are good weapons we're building, comrades!"

★ ★ ★

WHILE THE K-19 WAS PREPARING for her first major exercise, Soviet political directorates were busily broadcasting propaganda showing their navy was equipped with new atomic-powered submarines which, like the widely acclaimed U.S.S. *George Washington*, were capable of patrolling off the United States coast. It was also reported that they were capable of striking cities with atomic-tipped missiles launched undetected from submarines patrolling deep in North Atlantic waters. Russian television showed moving picture footage carefully doctored to show missiles being launched from submerged submarines billed as superior to American submarines. The navy and Strategic Rocket Forces were displayed repeatedly to the public as the bastions of homeland defense. In a society in which new military hardware was rarely shown to the public, the pictures of submarines and strategic missile launchers were amazingly current and were fed continually to the populace in an attempt to mask the real state of Soviet defense insufficiency. The protests of Zateyev and others like him were still cries in the wilderness.

THE REACTOR ACCIDENT

CHAPTER SIX

THE NUCLEAR ACCIDENT ABOARD the *K-19* on July 4, 1961, is one of the most horrific stories in the history of the sea. Captain Zateyev and his crew were submerged off the coast of Greenland, 1,500 miles away from their home port, participating in a widely publicized display of atomic submarine superiority. In a rare break with tradition, the military exercise had been reported to the Soviet public as it was unfolding with a great deal of fanfare and bravado. The navy had, in the words of the propagandists, reached not only parity with the United States but also had surpassed its rival with larger, better, and longer-range weapons. Then a pipeline in the primary cooling loop for *K-19's* reactor number one ruptured.

Heroic measures would be taken. Brave sailors would expose themselves to unheard-of levels of deadly radiation. And the lives of all aboard would be forever seared. But the underlying gravity of the *K-19* catastrophe reached far beyond the broken reactor and the swollen bodies of crewmen cooked by radiation. The failure of its cutting-edge weapons systems would seal the fate of a Soviet misadventure begun a year later when Premier Nikita Khrushchev gambled that he could make up for the lack of an accurate long-range nuclear capability by covertly deploying his inferior weapons to the advance base of Cuba, the Soviet Union's new ally in America's backyard.

The experience of *K-19* in the North Atlantic in July 1961 was not the first reactor mishap to befall the submarine force. Several casualties with the reactor primary cooling loops had already occurred but had been concealed to prevent punishment of those involved. The *K-5*, the second atomic attack submarine of the same class as the celebrated prototype *Leninsky Komsomol K-3*, experienced fuel-element cracks that resulted in the replacement of a reactor. *K-8*, the third attack boat of the same class, suffered a ruptured tube in a steam generator in October 1960 that seriously irradiated 13 crewmen, some of whom subsequently died. That boat eventually sank ten years later following a fire in a reactor space, taking 52 crewmen to their deaths. The casualties experienced by Zateyev in July 1961 were serious enough and so widely known that they caused the fleet command to modify all reactors with backup cooling systems.

★ ★ ★

ZATEYEV WAS TAKING his men to sea for a showcase exercise and trial operational missile shoot. The *K-19* would participate in a month-long exercise during which it would be hunted by other submarines, all conventional diesel boats. The maneuvers would culminate with the live launch of one of its ballistic missiles into the barren Novaya Zemlya target range to the north. The *K-19* would attempt to proceed through a large antisubmarine warfare barrier undetected, escape under the Arctic ice cap, surface through the ice, and launch one of three missiles from its silo built into the after portion of the sail. This exercise was a major event for the new submarine force, a trial exercise for the atomic sailors, and a strategic display for the Soviet Union.

A large number of the Northern Fleet and Moscow main navy staff officers would be in the exercise area aboard a cruiser observing the beginning of the exercise. Following several days of maneuvers, *K-19* would steam at covert speed to reach the relative safety of the Arctic ice pack. Then with a new adversary, the sub would pick its way through the dangerous ice cap, find the way to a thin spot in the ice, hover nearby, then, at the appointed time, surface through the ice and fire its missile. The sub would then head home.

★ ★ ★

ON JUNE 1, 1961, I was summoned to fleet headquarters in Severomorsk and was received by Fleet Commander Chabanenko. He had decided to concentrate the coming fleet exercises entirely on our forces' antisubmarine capabilities. My own ship, the *K-19*, was to play the role of the "adversary." Her mission was as follows. Undetected by NATO ASW forces, she was to enter the Atlantic, take up a waiting position, and at a signal from Moscow proceed through the Denmark Strait, transiting through it under ice, then follow the zero meridian north under the ice sheet, round Spitsbergen from the north, enter the Barents Sea, and at a command from shore, inflict a nuclear missile strike on a battlefield in Mezen Bay. Estimated time at sea: one month. We were to maintain concealment measures the entire time, breaking radio silence only in exceptional circumstances. We would take standard combat munitions, with a single practice missile (two out of our three ballistic missiles were real war shots).

The ship was to be completely ready by June 15. I was ordered to report our readiness to put to sea personally on the 16th. I left fleet headquarters feeling proud of the responsibility I'd been handed. For nearly the entire 100-kilometer trip back home I thought about what a load I was carrying now and how I was going to manage it all.

Almost everything was going to be new: a new crew, a new mission of national importance—to show what our nuclear atomic fleet was capable of—and finally the unseen rivalry with NATO's submarines. There was a great deal riding on us, and everyone understood this, from seaman to commander.

The crew was briefed on our mission, and we began readying our ship for patrol. We had to study our intended route thoroughly. The first obstacle we would have to overcome would be the Lofoten Archipelago, an area constantly patrolled by Norwegian antisubmarine forces. I knew that the Norwegians had laughed at our diesel submarines back in 1956, and we had to be prepared. We inspected all of the topside superstructure, battening down whatever might rattle or clatter, throwing out whatever we could and so on. We spruced up the propeller blades by cleaning them of sea growth and polishing them to smoothness. We exchanged our food provisions for a better grade.

The next ASW barrier we would have to get past was at the Faeroe-Iceland Gap. We knew that when large numbers of our ships left home waters, NATO air surveillance and patrolling by surface vessels would be stepped up in our exercise area. We decided to cross this barrier at its midpoint and at maximum operating depth.

The Denmark Strait looked like a tough passage. According to our current and projected charts it was obstructed by pack ice, which had begun moving south with the Greenland current and had completely covered over the strait. Worst of all, this year icebergs as thick as a kilometer had begun converging from the coast of Greenland in great masses. This was positively hazardous, because our *Arktika* acoustic sonar system couldn't penetrate farther than ten cable lengths. We decided to make some tests once we arrived in the area. After emerging from the Denmark Strait into the open waters to the south of Jan Mayen Island, we would proceed without fear of colliding with deep-draft icebergs until we had carried out our primary mission, which was launching the ballistic missile. We plotted our track and found it would take us an entire month before we arrived at "H hour," the launch point.

Next, we focused our attention on the equipment. We carried out a thorough regularly scheduled preventive maintenance-and-inspection routine. We were particularly concerned with our reactor's fourth cooling loop, which had been unreliable recently. To be prepared in case a leak developed in it, we gathered a supply of pipe repair fittings and other gear. On June 10 we started up both reactors. We checked out all systems and instruments. If anything looked even slightly doubtful, we replaced it. On June 12 we put to sea for 24 hours. Everything worked impeccably. We wouldn't have to worry about the equipment.

We spent June 13 and 14 loading the actual exercise missile, which was already prepared. We tested it for proper functioning, and everything worked perfectly. We were ready to put to sea.

On June 16 I left to deliver my personal report to the fleet commander. I found him in a pleasant mood. He warned me about the situation in the Denmark Strait and also said that the excitement in Polyarny was so great that you'd think nothing at all had ever happened there before. He wished me luck, and we said our good-byes. Our departure was scheduled for 1600 on June 18, 1961.

Several liaison officers from fleet headquarters came aboard for the exercise, including Captain Second Rank Vasily A. Arkhipov, plus a representative of the fleet's political directorate, Captain Second Rank Nikolai P. Andreyev. Literally minutes before we left port, two officers representing the brigade commander arrived on board. These were Captain Second Rank Vladimir F. Pershin, the commander of Crew 184, the reserve crew, and Captain Third Rank Georgy A. Kuznetsov, his executive officer. Both of these men were joining the mission at Sorokin's personal request as interns, to gain experience. We were supposed to take no more than an additional 10 percent of the number of our assigned crew, but these two officers put us above our maximum: We had 139 men on board when we sailed. Precisely on schedule, at 1600 on June 18, our submarine put to sea.

At 10 p.m. we submerged. It was decided that we would cruise at a depth of 150 to 160 meters. We would ascend to periscope depth to receive radio transmissions according to a fixed schedule, every 12 hours. For the first day at sea we worked on settling into our everyday procedures, concentrating chiefly on changes of watch, meals, and so on. By the second day we had settled comfortably into the routines of life aboard a navy ship.

We crossed the Cape Nordkyn-Bear Island barrier at a depth of 150 meters. According to our information, this barrier was not yet equipped with hydroacoustic detection arrays of the American Sound Surveillance System, or SOSUS, nor was it patrolled by ASW ships or aircraft. We had the Lofoten Archipelago on our port quarter. During a radio reception session, a visual scan of the surface didn't turn up a single ship. Essentially, we slipped into the Western Hemisphere undetected. We crossed the Faeroe-Iceland Rise with extreme caution, since this area was actively patrolled by ASW ships and planes. We descended to 250 meters, slowed to six knots, and periodically cut the engines. After exiting this area, we turned southwest.

On June 28 we reached the area southeast of Greenland where we were to wait. We kept to the eastern side of this area, since weather reconnaissance reported a major group of large icebergs on the western side. To the south lay a heavily trafficked shipping corridor between Europe and America. During one of our regular ascents to periscope depth, we carefully scanned the ocean surface. The skies were completely overcast, but visibility was excellent. We saw the famous East Greenland Current in action: A ridge of ice mountains loomed on the horizon. I decided to proceed awhile at periscope depth.

Passive sonar wasn't picking up a thing, and the horizon was clear. We could look out at the world through our periscopes. We swerved to get a closer view of one particular iceberg, for I had never seen such a huge mass of ice in my life. Keeping a safe distance of about 15 cable lengths, we circled it. I let everyone who wanted a look at this amazing sight have a turn at a periscope. It took us about ten hours to round the iceberg, and almost everyone had a look. We submerged again as soon as we detected an extremely faint signal from another operating sonar station.

June 30 was my 35th birthday. The senior cook midshipman, Mikhail Ivanchikov, made us some wonderful ice cream for that night, and I authorized servings of 100 grams of wine, doubling the daily ration. The officers wished me a happy birthday, and my second in command wished me a happy birthday on behalf of the crew over the ship's general announcing system. I also got a personal radio message from shore. It included a report on current conditions in the Denmark Strait. It was completely obstructed by ice and icebergs.

Off Angmagssalik, Greenland, ASW ships were actively searching for submarines, but they were unable to operate past the edge of the ice. There was no threat from aircraft patrolling above the ice. While crossing the strait we were instructed to take all possible precautions when encountering icebergs. I sent a coded signal to shore consisting of two letters. Literally only a minute later I received my "receipt" for this transmission.

We submerged to 150 meters, and on July 1 precisely at midnight we left our holding area and headed for the strait. By my calculations, we would be nearing the edge of an unbroken ice field in about 24 hours. Our depth was 200 meters, speed ten knots.

Once we passed under the edge of the ice, we set our sonar to scan ahead of our bow on a search sector of five degrees either side. From time to time we switched on the under-ice sonar as well. The *Arktika-M* sonar station was very effective at short distances. Its reflected "echo" was clear, which meant that we would have no difficulty detecting any icebergs dead ahead, and we'd have plenty of room to avoid them. I stationed myself in the sonar cubicle in order to train my watch officers and other commanders in iceberg avoidance. Our first encounter came at a speed of ten knots when the sonar-man reported an echo dead ahead, range 7.5 cable lengths (1,650 meters)!

The watch officer ordered, "Stop port turbine! Hard left rudder! Sonar, track target!"

I altered course 90 degrees to port, putting the target dead astern, and held that course for five minutes, then resumed our base course. (Left rudder or right rudder doesn't matter, the important thing is to act fast.) I restarted the port turbine. Not bad, I thought. I had decided to remain in the central command post until we'd had our first encounter with an iceberg, and it happened after only about 24 hours. Everything had gone exactly as per our training.

I drilled my watch officers and commanders often in iceberg avoidance. The drill routine was as follows: Initial speed, ten knots; the sonar man reports an echo dead ahead, range 7.5 cable lengths. The watch officer orders, "Stop port turbine. Hard left rudder. Sonar, track target."

They were getting it down. I decided to remain in the central command post until we'd had our first real encounter with an iceberg, which didn't happen until our second day out. We had no trouble at our next encounter with our "implacable foe," either; we evaded him easily. Passing Angmagsalik, we heard faint sonar transmissions, but there was no way to monitor them. If we spent more than 30 seconds in direct listening mode, we might miss the approach of an iceberg. So, after nearly 48 hours under way, my watch officers had thoroughly mastered iceberg avoidance, and I retired to my cabin for a few hours with no concern for the ship.

After we turned to a heading of 010 there were no more icebergs. We had changed our depth to 100 meters when there was a report: minor seawater leak in the reactor's fourth cooling loop. At 0330 on July 4, I decided to ascend to periscope depth for radio reception—it had been 72 hours since we'd last come up. I set general quarters. The navigators were prepared to fix our position; the Albatross radar station was on stand-by status. As we came to periscope depth, the surface was almost calm, with a moderate swell. We saw through the periscope that the horizon was clear. We made a few sweeps with the Albatross radar: nothing.

I stood down to Watch Condition Two. The navigators fixed our position, and found we were off track by about a mile and a half. We copied the scheduled radio broadcast; there were no messages for us. Thereupon we descended to 100 meters.

Captain Lieutenant Yuri Mukhin, Commander of the Missile Department, now came on watch. Captain Lieutenant Vladimir Pogorelov, Engineering Department Head, took over as duty engineer. Captain Second Rank Vasily Arkhipov, a diesel-power man but an experienced submariner, took the conn. The Number Two reactor control panel was manned by Senior Lieutenant Aleksandr Kovalyov, Number One by Senior Lieutenant Yury Yerastov. For now everything was normal. I retired to my cabin in Compartment Two.

★ ★ ★

THE ACTIONS IMMEDIATELY LEADING to the accident are reconstructed here based on written accounts as well as interviews with and testimony from survivors.

Lieutenant Yuri Povstyev, a 28-year-old engineer aboard the *K-19*, had worked around the clock for almost two weeks to keep this prototype submarine running safely, during its first test firing of the missile system at sea in real conditions. Yuri was the main propulsion engineer, in charge of the two 70-megawatt VM-A pressurized-water reactors. He was also responsible for the main engines and the all-important steam generators, where the primary coolant thermal energy from the two reactors' internal fission process was converted into steam to run the ship's power plant. To Yuri the steam generators were the mysterious part of the nuclear plant. The amazing generators were just complex heat exchangers where hot fluid passed energy to circulating water which, in turn, made steam and drove the turbines, imparting 39,000 horsepower to the two counter-rotating submarine propellers, driving the 4,000-ton steel hulk through murky Atlantic depths.

In principle, this submarine power plant was the same as any conventional steam-driven ship. Yuri knew that inside these giant steam generators was the forbidden boundary between the highly lethal radioactive liquid and the clean, saturated steam, which he knew and understood. The process inside the steam generators was shielded with heavy material that protected the vulnerable skin and organs of the human engineer from penetration by poisonous radiation. Yuri found it difficult to imagine that anything he could not see or feel could be of mortal danger to the body.

Early on the morning watch of July 4, while *K-19* was steaming homeward, 100 meters down in the depths of the North Atlantic, Yuri stood peering at the panel in Main Engine Control. He had been up the entire night trying to repair the emergency diesel generator, which for some reason had been unable to carry the full electrical load since they left port. Yuri knew they would need the diesel again soon, and he had caught up enough on the maintenance problems to think of getting some sleep.

Yuri took a cup of tea from one of the oncoming members of the engineering watch. He held the steaming cup and glanced once more over the panel of gauges and dials. The hot tea was good; it helped him relax. The humming vibrations from the deck plates felt soothing to his aching feet. He was tired. His gaze remained on the diagram for a moment—a line drawing of the steam cycle, placed overhead above the panel for quick reference. The left part of the diagram showed the twin reactors, red lines depicting the primary hot coolant as red arrows darting to the right. Blue lines of secondary liquid extended from the turbine diagrams on the right and converged with the red. Those blue lines Yuri trusted and understood. He had full confidence in everything connected with the blue lines. The place where the red and blue lines merged in the oval-shaped containers he had grown to dislike intensely—the steam generators—heat exchangers where the atomic generation and conventional power plant met. Despite his intense study of the manuals, Yuri could not envision where the danger stopped and clean steam began.

Yuri was ready to pass the controls to the engineering watch officer and put his head down for a few hours when he stiffened, immediately alert. His heart began to pound. A needle in a gauge on the left began to vibrate and pivot counter-clockwise—it represented the primary coolant pressure in the port reactor inlet. The Number Two reactor emergency protection alarm energized with a screech, signaling the worst possible propulsion casualty—a sharp pressure drop in the reactor's cooling loop.

Yuri felt his bowels involuntarily relax. He froze, eyes on the coolant pressure and adjacent temperature gauges. The sudden drop in pressure meant the system was losing coolant, and that meant heat from the nuclear fission process inside the reactor could not be removed and transferred in the normal manner to the secondary coolant flowing inside the heat exchangers. Yuri knew that flow had to be renewed, or the fission process in the reactor core would go on uncooled and, if unchecked, that could lead to eventual meltdown of the nuclear fuel, causing a catastrophic thermal explosion. Incredibly, early Soviet atomic power plants had no backup system to restore cooling to a reactor in such circumstances.

Yuri seized the intercom mike dangling from the overhead on the end of a black cord. He keyed it and automatically summarized the reason for the alarm to Central Command in the submarine's Compartment Three and simultaneously to the Chief Mechanic, who was in his cabin. Yuri knew by heart the required steps to take and outlined them distinctly on the intercom, then pushed the mike away from him. He darted forward to the hatch leading to the reactor space.

"Ivan, bring the standby feed pump on the line." The two engineers disappeared into the space between the engineering control and the reactor. The primary coolant pumps squatted in the dim light, one already failing, its audible hum winding down. The other pump was theoretically in readiness to take over the load. In the event that the first failed, Yuri and Ivan knew the procedure; they began twisting valve handles furiously, cutting in steam to the pump's impeller.

Nothing happened. Yuri swore and kicked the manifold violently.

"When was the last time we ran a test on this pump? It's supposed to be done each mid-watch," he growled. Ivan just stared wide-eyed, hands extended upward. "Run through the cycle again!"

The two engineers, soaked with sweat, twisted and kicked, then gave up, panting, "Keep trying, I'll report to Main Control." Yuri turned and half attacked, half spun the control handle on the door and disappeared, closing the hatch with a loud clang. Ivan repeated the cycle, twisting and kicking the silent mass of steel and hissing steam. Nothing.

Ivan looked at the adjacent pump. It was slowing rapidly, wheezing and clanking. Steam poured out around the main crank shaft. He tried everything he knew to get it going again, but to no avail. He knew instinctively that there must have been a leak in the primary coolant line since the pumps could not attain a head of pressure.

Yuri knew, in principle, how to restore cooling to the reactor without the system's two pumps, although he had never tried it. The engineers had to enter the shielded reactor compartment and to fabricate a backup system by welding pipes together. This they would do by cobbling together a device that would cycle steam plant water from the boat's reserve feed tanks into the reactor. A kind of homemade cooling condenser.

The compartment had been evacuated by the watch. Number Two reactor was providing all the ship's propulsion to both engines and all electrical power. The submarine wallowed ahead, still at 150 meters, straining to rise to the surface. Number One reactor had to be cooled quickly before serious core damage occurred.

Yuri shuddered. It was unorthodox, but in the absence of a working backup system, it was the only thing left to try. Yuri knew how to jury-rig things; he was an expert at that. Entering the shielded cubicle of an active reactor at sea was unheard of by

ABOVE: Nikolai Zateyev as a cadet in the Higher Naval School in Baku, 1943.
Photo courtesy the Historical Museum of the Northern Fleet, Murmansk.

LEFT: Nikolai Zateyev as Captain First Rank in 1962. Captain Zateyev's widow, Antonina, gave this photograph to film director Kathryn Bigelow, who carried it as a talisman through the making of the movie. *Photo courtesy Kathryn Bigelow/Antonina Zateyev.*

ABOVE: The *K-19* at dock at Polyarny with reinforcement over the bow acoustic antennae for surfacing through thin ice. The crew musters on the pier prior to deployment. *Photo courtesy Peter Huchthausen/Arkadi Mikhailovski.*

LEFT: Captain Second Rank Vladimir Yenin, Executive Officer aboard the *K-19* during the fatal patrol in July 1961. RIGHT: Petty Officer Second Class Yevgeni Kashenkov, one of the engineers who helped rig the back-up cooling system on the *K-19*. He died of intense radiation exposure on July 10, 1961. OPPOSITE: Boris Korchilov as a naval cadet in Leningrad, 1955. He was one of the first radiation victims.

Photos courtesy the Historical Museum of the Northern Fleet, Murmansk.

ABOVE: Surviving crewmen, including Yenin and Kulakov, after the July 4, 1961, accident at Naval Hospital Number One in Leningrad. The crewmen suffered hair loss, among other side effects, due to their exposure to intense levels of radiation. *Photo courtesy the Historical Museum of the Northern Fleet, Murmansk.*

TOP: The disabled *K-19*, spotted after her second major accident in February, 1972, by a U.S. Navy P-3 aircraft from the Atlantic Command's Patrol Squadron 56 flying out of Keflavik, Iceland, about 900 nautical miles east-northeast of Newfoundland. BOTTOM: Another P-3 from Patrol Squadron 56 first sighted the submarine on February 29, 1972, while a Soviet tug attempted a tow in rough waters.
U.S. Navy photographs.

ABOVE: Another view of the disabled *K-19* off the coast of Newfoundland, March 1972, taken from a Nimrod aircraft of 42 Squadron RAF Strike Command. *Crown Copyright, Ministry of Defense, Royal Air Force photograph.*

western standards, however, even in the early days of nuclear power. To prevent a disastrous reactor fuel meltdown, and the possibility of a violent hydrogen explosion, Yuri and his engineers volunteered to crawl, two at a time, inside the small space atop the reactor where the control rods were located, a space barely large enough for the men to stand, filled with radiation from its deck plates atop and in contact with the heated reactor vessel. It was madness, but it was their only hope.

★ ★ ★

AT 0415 I GOT a message over the *Nerpa* ship's announcing system: "Pressure in the starboard reactor has dropped to zero. Pressurizer level is zero. Reactor power has dropped to zero. Captain, please report to the Central Command Post."

The thought flashed through my mind that if all that were true, then we were facing the most unexpected and dangerous calamity that could happen to a nuclear reactor: a rupture in the primary cooling loop. I quickly made my way to the CCP. Pogorelov reported: "The number one reactor has scrammed because of a pressure drop to zero. The control rods are also showing zero. The backup circulation pumps have kicked in, and the receiver flasks have been disconnected from the control rods. The number one primary loop main and auxiliary circulating pumps have stopped. Looks like a rupture in the loop."

I listened to him without saying a word, then ordered the engineering department commander and the propulsion division commander, Captain Lieutenant Yuri Povstyev, to report to the CCP. After I heard their reports, I ordered a radiation alert: "Emergency in Compartment Six!" Then I went to the control panel to see for myself the evidence of what could no longer be avoided now. Yerastov confirmed the situation with his own instruments.

We uncovered the cause: A primary loop rupture had occurred somewhere in a section of pressure pipeline that is in constant use when the reactor is functioning. Where exactly, we couldn't tell. This meant that the water being fed to the reactor by the make-up pumps wasn't getting through. We began seeing evidence of radioactivity in Compartment Six. The primary loop pumps refused to start up. The control panel operators and crew of the reactor compartment did everything called for to contain the accident and douse the reactor core with water. But the instruments showed steadily climbing temperatures in the coolant channels of the reactor. I concluded that our guess of a rupture in the primary loop was completely correct and that the accident was a serious one.

We had to take effective and decisive action: Douse the reactor core with water to reduce its temperature and prevent a meltdown of the reactor core. (Operating manuals included strict instructions to prevent overheating of the reactor core by any means possible; otherwise, a thermal explosion could occur.) But how could we feed water directly to the reactor core?

For the time being we were heading north, for home port, at a depth of 100 meters, making ten knots on reactor Number Two. Captain Third Rank Anatoly Kozyrev and Captain Lieutenant Povstyev analyzed our emergency at the control panel. They were joined by Kovalyov, Gorsov, Filin, Prokofyev, Yerastov, and Mikhailovsky. Boris Korchilov was in Compartment Six, since he was compartment commander. Everyone agreed that the most likely location of the seal failure in the primary loop was somewhere underneath the plant.

The optimal solution, and the one we settled on, was proposed by Yuri Filin. Kozyrev presented me with the basic idea. If the pressure pipeline from a T-4A make-up pump was connected to the pipeline from the reactor's air vent, cutting that pipeline out of the air purging system, then this new line could be used to feed water directly into the reactor core. (The air vent serves to purge air from the reactor core when the reactor is first filled with coolant, i.e., bidistillate water.) I approved this idea and told Kozyrev to identify suitable piping for the new line. I ordered Pogorelov to prepare a welding set. This task was taken on by petty officer electricians Viktor Strasets, Anatoly Kalyuzhny, Fyodor Tokar, and Sergei Gusev. We also had to surface.

I briefed the crew on our situation and the emergency measures in progress. An emergency signal was now obligatory; we had our latitude, longitude, and date all filled in. At 0605 we surfaced to decks-awash condition, and I ordered transmission of our emergency signal. But we were unable to transmit. The insulation of our *Iva* (long-range, high-frequency "willow") antenna was completely flooded, and therefore shorted out. So one more part had failed. An incredibly important part too: The ship was now without any means of communicating with headquarters! We could chalk this failure up to prolonged submersion at great depths.

★ ★ ★

EVERY SOVIET SUBMARINE OF that era was equipped to send an encrypted emergency signal in times of distress. The signal was designed to contain certain basic data such as position and a brief explanation of the emergency, i.e., fire or flooding. The message was compressed electronically and sent in a burst transmission to lessen the likelihood of detection and fixing by NATO surveillance forces. Zateyev was unable to send his distress message due to the shorted antenna. The unusual movements of Soviet merchant ships and other combatants participating in the exercise were detected by U.S. naval intelligence converging on a single spot, causing NATO to dispatch surveillance aircraft to the scene to investigate the source of the emergency.

★ ★ ★

THE RADIATION READINGS for Compartment Six now showed 0.25 roentgens. The count for the other compartments was still normal. At last a suitable length of pipeline was found; the torpedo crew had come up with one suitable for the high temperature and pressure. We surfaced fully, maintaining our course for home, speed ten knots. I did not cancel the alert. I decided to tour the ship and try to buck up the crew. We definitely had a radiation problem. The temperature in the reactor coolant channels was still climbing. The indicator needles on the ASIT-5 (automatic coolant feed flow control system) panel were hitting their pegs, which meant that the temperature in the main feed lines had risen past 400 degrees C, more than twice their normal reading. In Compartment Six, the men were getting the welding equipment and pipeline ready to install a replacement cooling system by the time I finished making my rounds of the compartments.

I was deeply concerned. The worst problem now was that our communications were out. Captain Lieutenant Lermontov, the Communications Officer and Commander of Department IV, was doing everything possible, and there was no point in blaming him.

Events were by then slowly taking a turn for the worse. In Compartment Six, work began on rigging a new cooling system under the direction of the officer in charge, Senior Lieutenant Krasichkov. The crew cut the line leading from the reactor air vent and extended the new pipeline to where it would be joined to the air vent. An attempt was made to strip out coolant from the reactor compartment upper-level sump using the special 2P-2 pump, but the pump was air bound and could not gain suction because the heat had boiled the coolant to steam in the sump.

Accompanied by Captain Third Rank Kozyrev, I went to the compartment to observe the men's progress. (And let's face it: If you're sending men to their deaths, you have to reassure them. You have to let them know, if only by the presence of their commander, that they're not alone.) I was politely asked to leave the compartment, since radiation conditions made it hazardous to remain there for any length of time.

Once I'd made sure that the effort was well organized and proceeding apace, I decided to let the men do their jobs, without interference, and continued with my rounds of the submarine. Meanwhile, at the insistence of Captain Lieutenant Nikolai Vakhromeyev, the men working in Compartment Six were made to wear oxygen-breathing apparatus, or OBA. Vakhromeyev prepped each OBA himself, connected its air tube, tested it by giving it a couple breaths, then handed it in to the compartment.

Here is how the mood of the men working in Compartment Six was described by Senior Lieutenant Krasichkov: "During one shift, Ordochkin asked me how hot the reactor was now and whether an explosion was possible. He seemed embarrassed, as if ashamed to be worrying about these things; he was not in the least afraid. I reassured him as best I could by telling him the readings I was getting on the instrument panel. That's the sort of men they were! While working inside the reactor compartment, of course, they were alarmed, but they walked into that compartment without hesitation, ready for hard work. I saw the same calm, the same self-possession in Ryzhikov, Kashenkov, Penkov, Kharitonov, Savkin, and Starkov."

It seems that what really determines the choices a man makes in critical, life-threatening situations is still his inner conviction, his sense of responsibility for the events around him, his personal conscience. This is equally true of both the ones who send others to their deaths and the ones who go. Lieutenant Boris Korchilov came up to me and asked permission to assist in Compartment Six. All I said was, "Boris, do you know what you're asking?"

He answered firmly: "I know, Comrade Commander."

There is nothing I can add to this.

An initial attempt to butt-weld the two pipelines together failed. At that point, a short length of pipe was found that was larger in diameter than the two lines being joined, and it served as a coupling. The pipe from the air vent was inserted in one end, and the pipe from the T-4A booster pump went into the other. The edges of the coupling were then welded to the two pipelines.

This weld was a success—but at what a price! During the last phase of the welding operation in Compartment Six, the men working there reported that fire had broken out, with flames of a light blue to violet color appearing over the reactor lid. On orders from the Central Command Post, Compartment Six was sealed. Fires broke out twice, and they were extinguished with equipment that had been readied for this purpose in advance. But why a *violet* flame? I wondered.

Finally, the welding was finished, and the booster pump was activated. (It had been connected to a 30-ton tank of fresh water.)

I went below and made my way to Compartment Six. Standing at the bulkhead were Kozyrev and Vakhromeyev, who reported the situation. As they did so, the bulkhead door opened and Korchilov emerged from the compartment. He ripped off his gas mask and immediately began vomiting a white and yellow foam. He was taken to Compartment One, where a medical post had been set up. All the men who had been in Compartment Six were exposed to massive amounts of radiation, the doses they sustained going far beyond permissible levels.

We had to try to drain the forward reactor upper-level chamber sump. The main stripping pump for Compartment Eight failed; it was out of order. We decided to drain the sump with the main drainage pump for the central post. As soon as we started pumping, the radiation count rose in Compartments Five, Four, and Three. Evidently, particulate fission products were being flushed out with the sump water and channeled through these other compartments by the main drainage pump.

I felt my gorge rise. I went off to my cabin and lay down on my berth. Thoughts of all kinds were racing through my head. But I knew I had to take action. The problem now was how to save the crew and the ship. My main worry was the men. Everyone who'd been in Compartment Six was doomed; that much I knew already. But what could I do now? We were still about 1,500 miles from home. If we maintained a speed of ten knots, we'd arrive in six or seven days. We'd all be exposed to ten roentgens per hour at the very least for that entire period. That meant none of us would survive.

I remembered that during my pre-exercise briefing by the fleet commander, I'd happened to notice that his chart showed a screen of opposing diesel subs at the Iceland-Faeroe Gap. (I wasn't really supposed to know about them, since our *K-19* was on the "Blue" side, while the screen of diesel subs was "Red.") If those boats are still there, I thought (and I didn't know their exact coordinates), then we might still have a chance. But what if they'd been repositioned or even withdrawn altogether?

I agonized over what to do next: Turn south, where there was a small chance of joining up with the diesel subs and saving the crew, or proceed to base and bring the ship home with her crew dead. I climbed into the cockpit bridge and looked at the horizon. Not a ship in sight. I ordered the helm: "Right rudder, course 180°."

My decision was a carefully considered one. I was firmly resolved to attempt a rendezvous with our ships. The risk was enormous, but this was the only choice I could make.

★ ★ ★

ZATEYEV'S DECISION TO ATTEMPT to intercept the diesel submarine formation was a well-calculated judgment. He would rendezvous with other submarines whose radar profiles were small and difficult to detect on the surface. It was at this juncture that resistance appeared on the part of some officers, especially the senior Captain Pershin, who had been sent along on the exercise as a commanding officer of a reserve crew, but whose own experience and qualifications had been questioned by Zateyev. The choice of action preferred by Pershin and several others, who were frightened of the increasing radiation spreading throughout the boat, was to head for the nearest land, the Norwegian-owned island of Jan Mayen, which housed a NATO radar surveillance post. That option would mean beaching and abandoning the submarine in order to save lives, regardless of the fact that the land was Norwegian-owned. Deadly clouds of nuclear contamination would have covered the island, as crewmembers tried in vain to escape the radiation. Interviews with survivors have referred to this critical juncture in various terms ranging from concern, shared by some officers, to an outright attempt at mutiny.

★ ★ ★

I CALLED SENIOR LIEUTENANT Lermontov to join me in the cockpit and ordered him to prepare the small transmitter (a reserve, low-power unit). I instructed the cryptographer, Chief Petty Officer Aleksei Troitsky, to update our latitude and longitude in the text of each hour's radio report and transmit it every ten minutes. During scheduled copying of submarine support broadcasts he was to transmit those reports throughout the communications session.

I went below to announce my decision to the crew over the intercom, then returned to the cockpit. The small backup transmitter we were forced to use had a range of only about 50 miles. Would we find any Russian submarines?

Some time later Senior Lieutenants Vladimir Chersov (the commander of the reactor control group) and Mikhailovsky (the commander of the instrumentation and automation group) came up to the cockpit to meet with me. They demanded to know why we were going south into the unknown rather than heading for Jan Mayen Island, the nearest land. I heard them out. Then I sent them back down to do their duty. Their nerve had evidently failed them, and I felt sorry for them. They were the only ones who ever demanded such explanations of me.

Radiation conditions continued to deteriorate. I summoned my starpom, Captain Lieutenant Yenin, to the cockpit and authorized him to give the entire crew 100-gram servings of liquor. I knew that under the influence of alcohol (which is also a narcotic) the cells of the body are less susceptible to radiation; in other words, resistance to external irritants goes up. (Winos who are really drunk can withstand freezing temperatures and even beatings and other abuse.) On the strength of my experience of an accident in Obninsk, when an operator had dosed himself up on liquor before going to work on a reactor core and radiation had not affected him, I authorized this measure. For another thing, I thought, it wouldn't do any harm to give the men a shot of "liquid courage." Seaman A. I. Babchenko went a bit overboard, though, and had to be taken to sick bay.

Then I summoned my missile department commander, Captain Lieutenant Mukhin, and ordered him in Yenin's presence to gather the small arms (assault rifles and pistols) and throw them overboard, keeping only five pistols: for the commander, the starpom, Captains Second Rank Andreyev, Arkhipov, and Mukhin himself. This order was intended to discourage any attempts against my authority and was carried out immediately.

We steamed south for about ten hours on the surface. We never raised headquarters on the radio and didn't encounter a single ship, not even fishing vessels. Below decks, anxieties were running high. Would the newly repaired cooling system hold up? At one point a leak did develop in the jury-rigged piping. My starpom, Yenin; Chief Petty Officer Ivan Kulakov; and Seaman Leonid Berezov (the commander of the missile operators' department) repaired that leak and received heavy doses of radiation in the process.

According to my figures, by now we should have been in the diesel submarines' operating area. But no one had responded to our signals. Had I bet wrong? With a heavy heart I ordered the helm to reverse our course and then withdrew to my cabin. Yet not two minutes later I heard a report: "Silhouette bearing 270 degrees!"

I ran up to the cockpit and looked through my binoculars. I could clearly make out a stubby pole in the distance. I knew from experience that this could only be a submarine steaming directly for us. I gave the command, "Fire signal flare!" and ordered the helm, "Left rudder, heading 270 degrees."

The contact I'd seen was the S-270, a Project 613 submarine commanded by Captain Third Rank Jan Sverbilov. I will not describe the emotions I felt upon seeing one of our submarines. The gamble had paid off. The crew was saved.

★ ★ ★

AS CAPTAIN SVERBILOV ABOARD the S-270 approached the K-19, he carefully monitored the radiation coming from the stricken submarine. Two hundred yards away, the radiation was 0.4 to 0.5 roentgen per hour, increasing to 4 to 7 roentgens per hour as they had pulled alongside. A transfer between two submarines at sea is always tricky, as submarines roll and pitch considerably while on the surface. It was impossible to rig a gangway between the two ships, and so finally Captain Zateyev had the *K-19's* bow planes extended while Captain Sverbilov maneuvered the *S-270's* bow underneath the extended bow planes to provide a platform for the transfer.

Once the eight most seriously irradiated men were brought aboard the *S-270*, the radiation levels in Compartment One rose to 9 roentgens per hour. When Captain Sverbilov reported this to Captain Zateyev, the latter quickly recognized the problem: The injured men's clothing was highly contaminated. The men were stripped and their clothing thrown overboard. When they measured the radiation levels in the *S-270's* forward torpedo room again, they still read 0.5 roentgen per hour. The men themselves were radioactive. They had inhaled and swallowed enormous quantities of radioactive contamination that continued to irradiate both them and everyone around them even after they had left the *K-19*. The nuclear demon was loose.

Aboard the *K-19*, the engineers were busy shutting down the operating reactor. To provide electric power for the ship with the reactor shut down, they started one of the ship's two 400-kilowatt diesel generators. Aboard *S-270*, Captain Sverbilov again noted an increase in radiation. The diesel engine, drawing contaminated air from inside the crippled *K-19*, was spewing radioactivity in its exhaust.

★ ★ ★

FINALLY WE GOT A RADIO MESSAGE. "Commander of submarine *S-159*: The submarine *S-268* commanded by Lieutenant Captain Gennady Nefedov is proceeding to the accident site. You are instructed to give him custody of the *K-19* and proceed to base at maximum speed." A couple of hours later, we were on our way home.

Off North Cape we rendezvoused with the destroyer *Byvaly*. It was commanded by an old pal of mine from special naval high school and the Academy, Captain Second Rank Vladimir Sakharov. I bid the commander of the *S-159* a hearty farewell.

Once we transferred from the submarine to the destroyer, we immediately found ourselves in the hands of the dosimetrists and chemists. We were all thoroughly decontaminated; a number of us had to go through decontamination a second or third time to "wash off the roentgens." The petty officer working on me clapped me on the shoulder and said, "So what's next, buddy, you get released early from the navy?" (In a group of naked men, you can't tell an officer from a seaman.) I told him, "Probably so," and smiled.

We were given white sailors' jumpers to put on. The only thing that now distinguished me from the men was the pistol I still wore.

It took three days for us to reach home port. The day we came ashore the weather was fair; the sun was out, not a breath of wind. The storm had ended long before. The surface showed only a low swell out of the north. The ship slowly approached the mooring wall at Polyarny. The destroyer's berth was surrounded by troops with assault rifles. Beside the soldiers were ambulances. We were met on shore by the fleet commander, Admiral Chabanenko, and the head of the navy's medical service, Major General Tsypichev. The fleet commander had no questions for me. He was well aware of the tragic position we were in now.

The whole town of Polyarny had come out to meet our ship, forming a frightened and subdued crowd behind the line of soldiers. In wartime this was how the public would meet ships returning from battles.

I broke the silence with Admiral Chabanenko and asked him, "What's going to happen to me now?" He replied, "Right over there is the head of the Special Department, in this case a security detachment (probably headed by the naval intelligence branch of the KGB). Go and ask him." The man he'd indicated was Captain Second Rank Aleksandr Narushenko. He and I had had adjacent bunks on the submarine tender *Magomed Gadzhiyev.*

Narushenko smiled and said, "Nothing's going to happen. You did everything right."

We were quickly loaded into ambulances and taken to the hospital, which was no more than 50 meters from the pier. The hospital was already prepared to handle the injured. We were all given beds in the appropriate wards (the administration had been asked not to separate us). After a short breather I went to look in on my injured men. They were now in a completely withdrawn state; I could tell that they had only hours to live.

The medical specialists had decided to send them to the Institute of Biophysics in Moscow. A young doctor, Angelina Susokova (now a corresponding member of the Academy of Medical Sciences), assured me that the institute would do everything possible to save their lives. The next day, the men were flown to Moscow. Two helicopters landed in the stadium next to the hospital. Before they were loaded into the helicopters, I went to say goodbye to Korchilov, Ordochkin, Kashenkov, Savkin, Penkov, and Kharitonov.

I approached Boris Korchilov first. My God, what a toll the radiation had taken! His face was red, his lips swollen, his tongue so thick he could barely talk, his eyes swollen shut. I bent down to him and told him that he and his comrades were being taken to Moscow, where the doctors would help them get back on their feet. In a whisper, he asked me to help him open one of his eyes so he could have a look at me. He also asked for some juice. I did as he asked: held one eye open and poured some juice from a teapot into his mouth, which he could hardly open. I barely managed to restrain my sobs as I told him goodbye. Then I stepped away from Boris to say farewell to the others.

The men were loaded on stretchers into two helicopters. The first one took off without incident. The second one snagged an electric power line with its rotor right after takeoff and crashed to the ground at the very edge of the seawall. This happened with the entire hospital staff looking on! The emotions each of us felt are indescribable. After all the horrors of radiation poisoning, here was yet another unexpected torment.

Fortunately, the landing was gentle and the helicopter remained intact. A third helicopter soon arrived; the men were transferred, and it took off for Safonovo, where a transport helicopter awaited them. We never saw a single one of those men alive again. They died fully conscious, complaining of terrible pain.

The next day, after all our tests had been processed, we were assembled in the hospital auditorium. Around a table on the stage sat the hospital's chief physician and Rear Admiral Babushkin, representing the Navy's Chief Political Directorate. The chief physician told us we'd all got off easy. There was no danger to our health, and we had nothing to be alarmed about.

The men who'd been evacuated to Moscow were in critical condition, but even their chances were far from hopeless.

The following days were crucial ones for me. From the very first day of our stay in the hospital at Polyarny, we were all terrorized by Rear Admiral Babushkin. He was after one thing only: to discredit the commander and accuse me of exceeding my authority by abandoning ship. Day in and day out he called my seamen, petty officers, and officers in to see him for "conferences," questioning each one exhaustively about his commander's conduct during the emergency. When they'd had as much of these "interrogations" as they could take, they declared that unless Babushkin was removed from the hospital, they would throw him out themselves, after first beating his face in. I reported this to the fleet commander during one of his daily visits to the hospital. After that, we never saw Babushkin there again.

A day after the chief physician's report to us, we got the news from Moscow that Lieutenant Korchilov, Petty Officer First Rank Ordochkin, and Petty Officer Second Rank Kashenkov had all died on July 10. Meanwhile, in Polyarny an investigation was launched. Some dubious persons began summoning us for questioning. I told them all exactly where they could go. On July 12 Seaman Savkin died. On July 13 Seaman Kharitonov died. On the 15th Seaman Penkov died. Everyone began thinking that the same fate awaited him, that it was only a matter of time—if not today, then tomorrow.

I began suffering terribly from insomnia. I'd already lost track of how many days it had been since I'd stepped off that ship, and I still couldn't put the thing out of my mind even for a moment. You can't imagine the kind of thoughts you find yourself brooding over. I remember asking Senior Lieutenant Krasichkov during a smoking break, "So, you think we'll end up trading in our hospital gowns for prison uniforms?" What was he supposed to say to *that?*

Meanwhile, the hospital was busy with us day and night, taking samples of everything the human body can possibly produce. We were divided into groups according to the severity of the radiation poisoning we had sustained. Two groups would be sent to Leningrad: The first, with the most severe exposures, would be taken by plane to the battlefield therapeutics department of the Military-Medical Academy. The second group, with moderately severe exposures, would be sent by train to Special Ward No. 11 of the First Naval Hospital (for treatment by the department of naval and hospital therapeutics). A third group, with the least severe doses, would be released after treatment and observation to convalesce at the Northern Fleet's rest-and-recuperation facility in Shchuk-Ozero. The first group departed on July 14; the second, my own group, departed the next day.

Before our departure for Leningrad, the head of the Navy's Chief Political Directorate, Admiral Grishanov, visited the hospital. He stopped by my ward for literally a few seconds, just long enough to thank me on behalf of the Party, the government, and navy command, for the fortitude and courage I had shown during the accident and to wish me a speedy recovery. I concluded that the investigation was over and that there had been a shift in official attitude toward me and my crew. Later, the government commission chaired by academician Anatoly Aleksandrov would find that the actions of the crew of the *K-19* in managing the reactor accident had been correct.

By a decree of the Presidium of the U.S.S.R. Supreme Soviet dated August 5, 1961, the personnel who took part directly in installing the emergency reactor cooling system and extinguishing the fires in the reactor chamber were decorated with medals, reading: "For Courage and Heroism." I myself was awarded the Order of the Red Banner. But this would all happen later.

For the time being, the crew faced long hospital stays for medical exams and treatment. We all had the same diagnosis: acute radiation sickness (of every degree of severity). The doses we'd sustained were determined by examination of the thyroid gland and also of the dry residue of stool samples (obtained by the method known as evaporating and "ashing"). We even allowed ourselves a bit of fun with this part: We would "help out" our neighbor. Two of us, for example, would make our own contributions to Pershin's daily measured output of urine and feces. The doctors and nurses would then wonder aloud how he could possibly have produced so much. We would say to them: "Have you seen the way he *eats?* A big man like Pershin—you've got to expect a big output."

What is radiation sickness actually like? What are the symptoms? The first signs are uninterrupted vomiting beginning about 15 to 20 minutes after exposure, with redness on unprotected areas of skin (radiation burns). After about one and a half to two hours there is massive edema. The whole body puffs up so badly that the eyes can no longer open. The tongue swells, making speech almost unintelligible. Ichor, a straw-colored serous discharge, begins running from the hair-covered areas, particularly the scalp. All of this is accompanied by agonizing pain and loss of mobility that continue without loss of consciousness until death. These, of course, are the symptoms of the most severe exposures. Smaller doses of radiation result in a latent early phase of the disease, in which the victim feels completely normal for a period of several days before symptoms appear.

Our seamen sustained varying degrees of radiation poisoning, ranging from extremely critical to minor cases. By this time medical science had already had the opportunity to develop a methodology for the treatment of radiation sickness. The fates of the men who'd taken the heaviest doses of radiation were already sealed: Korchilov, Ordochkin, Kashenkov, Savkin, Penkov, and Kharitonov all died. But the fates of the others lay in the hands of their doctors. They were treated by two methods that differed chiefly in the timing and choice of the initial treatment. One method began with bone-marrow transplants and proceeded to blood transfusions. The other began with blood transfusions and monitoring of the white blood cell count, and if the transfusions failed to arrest the process of white blood cell depletion, the next step was bone-marrow transplants. The first method restored the body's ability to form blood cells before all its systems were completely weakened, and thus restored general vitality; the second method in effect restored the life functions of a body that had been severely weakened. The first method saved the lives of Ivan Kulakov, Mikhail Krasichkov, and Vladimir Yenin, who are alive and well to this day. The second method cost the lives of Yury Povstyev and Boris Ryzhikov.

I should note that this experience ought to have played a fundamental role in the development of a school of radiation sickness treatment. And yet a surprisingly large number of fatal outcomes resulted from the Chernobyl tragedy. The

American doctor Robert Gale clarified this situation somewhat during his visit when he announced that we'd been following the wrong treatment plan and suggested substituting the method devised by Professor Volynsky!

Aboard the submarine *K-19* over three days passed before our men reached qualified medical attention at a hospital, but the Chernobyl victims were treated immediately following the accident. Is there any avoiding the conclusion that the suddenness of the disaster and the completely inadequate preparedness of our medical establishment were to blame for such large numbers of casualties?

At the Military-Medical Academy and the First Naval Hospital we sailors were treated with the most heartfelt kindness and attentiveness.

To our great sorrow, two more of our comrades could not be saved. Main Propulsion Officer Yuri Povstyev died on July 20 in the arms of Kozyrev and Yenin. Three days later Boris Ryzhikov also died. He fought fiercely for his life to the very end, never losing consciousness. And to think that when he was first transferred to the Military-Medical Academy, he was still well enough to play volleyball.

Our group in the hospital was assembled in the hospital auditorium around August 10 to receive government awards. Many seamen, petty officers, and officers received various decorations and medals, and the entire crew was presented valuable gifts from the Defense Ministry. The decorations and awards were presented by the commander of the Leningrad Naval Base, Admiral Ivan Ivanovich Baikov. Yet he not only failed to say anything that might have bucked up the men, he failed to say anything intelligent whatsoever. Instead, with a kind of casual air he said, "You all think you're some sort of heroes now, don't you? Listen, here in Leningrad we have accidents, too—streetcar accidents... ." I felt like taking the medal I'd just been given and flinging it right into that smug, arrogant, overfed face of his.

By tradition, courage is one of the qualities that distinguishes the officers and seamen of the Russian Navy. The problem is, everyone has his own view of what constitutes courage. On July 4, 1961, a fire broke out in a reactor compartment of a nuclear submarine of the Northern Fleet. The members of its crew, commanded by Captain 1st Rank Nikolai Vladimirovich Zateyev, successfully eliminated the danger this posed to their ship. The surviving crew members (but far from all of them) received government awards. After all that, Admiral Ivan Baikov, the commander of the Leningrad naval base, unbelievably said to these men, "You all think you're some sort of heroes now, don't you? Listen, here in Leningrad we have accidents, too—streetcar accidents... ."

On August 22 everyone who'd been in the hospital left for a stay at the rest-and-recreation facility in Zelenogorsk outside Leningrad, and on September 14 we all returned to the hospital. On September 27 we were examined by a military medical commission. We were all officially diagnosed as suffering from "asthenic vegetative syndrome." At the time, we were told that this was done to conceal the real diagnosis of radiation sickness, which couldn't be made public knowledge. ·Later I learned that "asthenic vegetative syndrome" refers to some sort of mental disorder and has nothing to do with radiation sickness at all. So they made mental patients of us! That's what you get for serving in the Navy!

On September 28 I was discharged from the hospital and left for Zapadnaya Litsa to assume my new post as deputy

commander of the 3rd Division of the Northern Fleet's 1st
Flotilla of nuclear submarines.

Petty Officer First Rank Ordochkin, Petty Officer Second
Rank Kashenkov, and Seamen Penkov, Savkin, and Kharitonov
are buried in Kuzmin Cemetery in Moscow. Captain Lieutenant
Yuri Povstyev and Lieutenant Boris Korchilov were laid to rest
in Krasnenkoye Cemetery in Leningrad. Chief Petty Officer
Ryzhikov was buried in the municipal cemetery of Zelenogorsk,
near Leningrad. A street in the northern town of Zaozyorny, the
residential center of our nuclear fleet, was renamed Lieutenant
Korchilov Street in honor of Lieutenant Boris Korchilov.

★ ★ ★

NOR WAS THAT THE end of the story for the *K-19* or the ships
that carried the crewmen home. The rescue ships, including
Captain Jan Sverbilov's *S-270*, all had to be carefully decontaminated upon reaching port. The *K-19* was towed back to port
by the Swedish-built *Pamir*-class ship *Aldan*, arriving around July
10. By the time she arrived, three compartments had flooded,
yet the ship was still afloat. The *K-19* lay tied up in port with
ventilation systems running, and radioactive material from the
inside of the sub contaminated everything within a 700-meter
radius: a hillside, buildings, equipment, plants, and people. The
authorities had decided to scuttle the ship near Novaya Zemlya,
but several of the crew members argued passionately that the
ship should be decontaminated and restored to service. In the
end, the volunteers managed to dewater the submarine, strip her
of all equipment and furnishings, and completely decontami-
nate the insides. The reactor compartment was replaced in its
entirety. Another heroic effort by brave men, partially motivated

by patriotism and partially acting out of naïveté, but the ultimate cost to those volunteers may never be known.

Had the *K-19's* makeshift cooling system failed to cool the reactor and the uranium fuel core's temperature continued to rise, a violent explosion would have followed. An explosion while submerged would have simply obliterated the *K-19*. An explosion while on the surface would have released a massive cloud of nuclear contamination, dwarfing the released radiation of the Chernobyl explosion. The resulting long-term effects are terrible to imagine. While there have been uncontrolled surges by runaway reactors, no naval reactor has ever reached the stage of total fuel meltdown.

For the men who lived through the terrifying event, the memories of their experience would stay with them for the rest of their lives. Institutional memory, however, would prove to be criminally short. The lessons learned from the accident were few. The greatest effort would be expended in covering up what happened. Only a long road of willful ignorance would lead from the *K-19* into the future.

 **C**APTAIN ZATEYEV DESCRIBED the actions that followed the investigation into his accident and how the senior members of the shipbuilding hierarchy and the navy operational command structure acted to protect their personal interests and did little to ensure that future accidents did not result from the same mistakes. The Navy Political Directorate was traditionally the first to offer the public information about naval accidents. In this case, the directorate never made a public announcement. The behavior over time of the directorate did not change, and when accidents such as the loss of the nuclear submarine *Komsomolets* occurred in April 1989, well into the Gorbachev period of glasnost, the Navy Political Directorate willfully made false statements to the Russian media covering up the serious nature of the loss of the reactor and two nuclear weapons.

This policy of suppressing information about nuclear accidents continued through the end of the Cold War into the post-Soviet Union era and included not only naval accidents but also all nuclear power mishaps. With the disintegration of the Soviet Union in 1991 and the extensive political reforms that followed, the large numbers of nuclear submarines and nuclear weapons were significantly reduced. In 1989 the Soviet Navy operated its largest number of nuclear submarines—a total of 196. The numerous disarmament agreements between the United States and Russia, including the Start I and Start II treaties, called for the drastic reduction of the numbers of strategic submarines and nuclear weapons. These rapid reductions required the immediate dismantling of hundreds of submarine nuclear power plants and nuclear weapons and the safe storage and processing of nuclear fuel and waste. The agreement provisions could not be adequately met because of the collapsing Russian economy and the lack of financial resources needed to comply. The same propensity to cover up the truth of the nuclear misfortune extended to the handling of nuclear waste and storage of nuclear fuel elements from decommissioned submarines, leading to one of the most dangerous problems confronting the 21st century. Accidents and near accidents have been occurring in Russian nuclear power plants for years, the most serious ones since Chernobyl being caused by the loss of electrical power and failure of backup emergency diesel power to continue cooling power plants. The most recent and dangerous of these episodes occurred in February 1993 when a Kola nuclear power plant, called Polyarnyy Zori—the first nuclear plant built above the Arctic Circle—went without cooling for two and a half hours. Natural circulation barely prevented a fuel core meltdown. Given the increase in importance of learning from past mistakes, the words in Nikolai Zateyev's memoir take on even greater meaning. What happened in the aftermath of the *K-19* accident would be repeated time and again, leading to the disaster at Chernobyl.

★ ★ ★

ON OCTOBER 13 AND 14, 1961, a high-level conference chaired by the First Deputy Commander in Chief of the Navy, Admiral Kasatonov, was held in Moscow. First I must explain how I wound up attending it. After our release from the hospital on October 9, we arrived at Zapadnaya Litsa to file the papers necessary for us to go on leave (both sick leave and regularly scheduled vacations). At the same time I was supposed to assume my new position: that of deputy commander of the 3d division of the Northern Fleet's 1st nuclear submarine flotilla.

There was no one whose duties I was supposed to assume— the entire staff had only just been appointed—and no one to take over my own duties as commander of the *K-19*. On October 11 I was ready to go. But I got a telephone call that day from the fleet commander, who told me that the next morning he and I would be flying to Moscow for a conference.

I had no idea what sort of conference it was going to be. Our flight took just over three hours (in the commander's IL-2), and we took rooms at the Central House of the Soviet Army Hotel. On the morning of October 13 the fleet commander and I went to navy headquarters. The conference was held in a small second-floor conference room. Every top leader in the field of nuclear shipbuilding, both military and civilian, was in attendance. I won't dwell on the remarks by the irresponsible ones; I was seeing most of them for the first time in my life.

The one man I did know was academician Anatoly Aleksandrov. And he was the only one who spoke out in defense of the crew of the *K-19*. Anatoly Aleksandrov described the actions taken by the crew of the *K-19* to manage the reactor accident as completely correct, repeatedly stressing the personal courage of the seamen, petty officers, and officers, and called for an end to the various speculations and insinuations against the *K-19*. He added that the adoption and development of nuclear energy was proceeding at a cost in terms of human lives *lower* than that of any comparable branch of science or industry. The other speakers shut their mouths.

The other academician attending the conference, Nikolai Dollezhal, preferred not to comment. This brought the debate to a close. During the long recess that followed, Anatoly Aleksandrov and Nikolai Dollezhal asked Admiral Chabanenko and me to join them "for a moment" at the hallway window to the right of the conference room door. There they showed us photographs of the rupture in the pulse tube and allowed us to read the conclusions of the accident investigation committee. The rupture of the tube was attributed to the following factors: During installation of the primary cooling loop pipelines, welding safety procedures had been violated. These procedures called for all surfaces to be covered with asbestos drop cloths in order to keep even a single drop or spark from a welding rod from falling on the polished surface of the pipelines. This rule was disregarded because of the cramped spaces in which the work was performed. Drops of liquid metal from the welding electrodes fell on an unprotected surface. Wherever those drops fell on the pipeline, i.e., its surface layer of metal, molecular tension developed and led to the appearance of micro cracks in the metal. When those micro cracks later came into contact with chlorides (seawater inevitably makes its way into the bilge and from there, as vapors, it enters recesses), the micro cracks gradually developed into ordinary cracks extending through the entire wall of the pipeline, forming so-called "plugs." The strength of the pipelines wherever drops fell on them from welding rods was thus greatly compromised. After prolonged and intensive operation of the reactor with coolant circulating through the primary loop under a high working pressure (200 atmospheres), a pressure gauge pulse tube finally ruptured. (The Institute of Physics and Energy proposed eliminating this molecular tension by polishing any areas hit by drops of metal from welding rods with "velour" emery paper or other materials.)

The photographs we were shown were of the rupture in the tube, shot from every possible angle. The inner diameter of the tube was 10 mm, with a wall thickness of 2.5 mm. The edges of the rupture were smooth. That was all Dollezhal said. As he showed us the ruptured tube, he didn't say a word about the consequences. He didn't say a word about the lack of an emergency reactor cooling system, or the fact that this was a design flaw.

I told Anatoly Aleksandrov how events had unfolded aboard the ship. I said that the decisions made had been firm ones. There had never been any hesitation. The destruction of the reactor had never been regarded as a possibility. The results of our efforts are on record. We acted in strict accordance with our instructions, and if we hadn't, if we had departed from them even for an instant, then no matter what happened to anyone else, the ship's commander and the commander of its engineering department would certainly have been court-martialed.

After the long recess it was my turn to address the conference. My remarks were brief. After noting my ship's positive characteristics, its autonomy in submerged mode, its speed and weaponry, I said that it was simply embarrassing to sail in ships that still needed as much work as ours did. Every single voyage ended in some kind of accident. Not one of our submarines ever returned to base without breakdowns and malfunctions. Steam generators were always flying to pieces, or the auxiliary pumps or main circulating pumps of the primary cooling loop would fail and so on and so forth. Meanwhile, the ships' noisiness completely wiped out any benefits from the advantages I'd mentioned earlier. And yet I personally, like all my fellow commanders, was not afraid to put to sea. (At the time I was still unaware that a smear campaign against the *K-19* was in progress.)

The major result of the conference of October 13-14, 1961, was as follows:

1. The reactors of all nuclear submarines then under construction or already commissioned were to be fitted out with *SOAR* emergency cooling systems (simply put, emergency reactor dousing systems).
2. A certain submarine was to be repaired, its Sixth Compartment replaced (the ship in question was the *K-19*).
3. After the conference, Fleet Admiral Chabanenko gave me leave to go and offered a final word of advice: "Rest up, and don't worry."

On March 30, 1990, the Rubin Production Association held a reunion conference for veteran sailors of the strategic nuclear-powered ballistic missile submarine fleet. The occasion was the 30th anniversary of the raising of the navy flag on the *K-19*. Two weeks earlier I had personally delivered an invitation to the conference to academician Anatoly Aleksandrov. He had accepted it gratefully. We got to talking and went on for a whole hour. Our conversation was frank, unconstrained (we had met in the academician's office at his institute in the Oktyabrskoye Polye area of Moscow). I was very curious to hear what the academician would say about the accident 30 years later. Finally, when the talk turned to Chernobyl, I couldn't resist any longer and asked him,

"Anatoly Aleksandrov, at this point, almost 30 years after the accident aboard the *K-19*, would you say that the situation on our ship was comparable to Chernobyl? Particularly since we saw a violet glow appear twice over the reactor lid, and fire broke out twice in the control room?" He considered his answer for a long time, then said precisely the following: "It could be that no explosion was going to occur."

(Incidentally, the control console logbook for the reactor involved in the accident disappeared without a trace while the government commission was deliberating, and all attempts to find it since then have failed. Someone clearly has an interest in keeping the entries in this logbook out of the public record.)

As for me, however much anyone argues that no explosion was imminent, I'd still like to know why it was nevertheless decided that all reactors thereafter, including the Chernobyl design, needed emergency cooling systems. And why hadn't an emergency cooling system been built into the first-generation ships?

Here is what Captain First Rank V. P. Zhukovsky wrote me: "Based on my direct involvement with issues stemming from submarine disasters, I have arrived at the conclusion that the crews of our operating nuclear submarines were not fully briefed on the events that occurred on your ship at the time. It was somehow implied that the decisions to go forward with emergency dousing of the reactor were made without a pre-liminary analysis of the condition of the primary cooling loop and the serviceability of the pumps. And not one word was said about the reactor control personnel continuing to regu-late the temperature in the core coolant channels through the ASIT-5 (automatic coolant feed-flow control system). I only learned about this myself last year when I read Pogorelov's account. Every following nuclear submarine of this series and all other designs were equipped with built-in emergency dousing systems (or emergency cooling systems, as they're also called). I can vouch for the accuracy of this information on the basis of personal experience, since as a division commander from January 1961 through 1964 and then as assistant force engineer officer for the next eight years developing accident-prevention measures with ships' crews, I made constant use (like everyone else) of this tragic experience in truncated form. The cause of the disaster aboard your ship was a design flaw in the steam plant. Many people are unaware of this."

I knew perfectly well that the facts were being concealed and falsified. This was done by people who disregarded what-ever conscience they had. And so we paid with young men's lives for the blunders and errors of our designers, specifically N. A. Dollezhal. The authorities had good reason to prohibit telling submariners why the accident occurred and why it resulted in fatalities.

The whole thing started back at Zapadnaya Litsa. Who ini-tiated this campaign? Anatoly Sorokin. He was evidently act-ing on orders—*whose* orders I still didn't know. But I'll return

ABOVE: Harrison Ford as Captain Alexei Vostrikov, the character based on Captain Nikolai Zateyev, proudly accepting his new assignment to command the prestigious *K-19*, pride of the Soviet fleet.

All photographs by George Kraychyk, courtesy of Intermedia and Paramount Pictures.

ABOVE: In the Command Center of the *K-19*, Harrison Ford's character, Captain Vostrikov, is brought aboard to replace the demoted Captain Polenin, played by Liam Neeson.

RIGHT: Liam Neeson as Captain Polenin.
BELOW: Political officer Igor Suslov, played by
Ravil Isyanov, becomes concerned about rising
radiation levels and the Captain's judgment.

RIGHT: Director Kathryn Bigelow, shown with Joss Ackland, who plays the Soviet Defense Minister, and John Shrapnel, who plays the Commander in Chief of the Soviet Navy, in a scene where the two men review the geopolitical implications of deploying the *K-19* in waters so close to the U.S..

LEFT: Most of the crew of the *K-19* (including Captain Vostrikov, played by Harrison Ford, on the conning tower) pose for a photograph after surfacing beneath the Arctic Circle.

BELOW: *K-19* crew members play a brisk game of soccer on the Arctic ice cap.

LEFT: J. J. Field plays Andrei, the cook, who provides comfort and sustenance for his comrades in the midst of the crisis.
BELOW: Michael Gladis plays an inexperienced young sailor who brings his pet mouse aboard with him.
TOP RIGHT: Assistant reactor officer Pavel Loktev, played by Christian Camargo, dons protective gear before heading into the sealed reactor chamber to attempt the initial repair of the failed cooling system.
BOTTOM RIGHT: Peter Saarsgard plays young reactor officer Vadim Radchentko, who suffers intense radiation exposure as he courageously attempts to repair the reactor's failed cooling system.

RIGHT: Harrison Ford defends his command of a troubled ship.
BELOW: Surviving officers from the *K-19* await questioning from a government inquiry about the accident.

to that later. What was the goal of the campaign? Whose interests did it serve? He ordered the officers of the brigade staff, and thereafter the staff of 31st Division, not to allow anyone to examine the materials developed by the government commission on the *K-19* accident (chaired by A. P. Aleksandrov), citing alleged orders from the leadership to keep these documents out of the public record. Later he would argue that he had been justified in doing so because an objective assessment of the accident might have frightened crew members out of serving in the nuclear fleet and because there was a need to uphold the authority of our shipbuilding industry and show that accidents like this one were chance events, not the result of design factors. The crew's actions were represented as not the ones called for by reactor operation protocol.

The smear campaign being orchestrated by Sorokin continued. After the brigade was reorganized into a flotilla, Sorokin was appointed commander of 31st Division, whose ships were reassigned to Bolshaya Lopatka. It was there that the members of the *K-19's* second crew erected with their own materials and labor a modest waterside memorial to the dead sailors along with a case displaying photographs of the seamen, petty officers, and officers of the first crew (29 men) who had received decorations. The sight of this memorial was intensely galling to Sorokin, and when he was appointed flotilla commander, which involved the relocation of 31st Division to Sayda Bay (Gadzhiyevo), he ordered it destroyed, saying, "I don't want to see one single reminder of *K-19* around this place *ever!*" About the only thing he couldn't do to make the humiliation of the *K-19's* crew complete was to get the name of Lieutenant Korchilov Street changed. Yet destroying the memorial went beyond blasphemy; it was even worse.

So who was this Sorokin? This "hero" rose to the crest of the nuclear wave thanks exclusively to his skill at rolling out the red carpet for his superiors. Before he was appointed commander of a division of nuclear submarines under construction in Severodvinsk, Sorokin had commanded a Project 613 diesel sub based in Paldiski (Estonia).

Apart from the exemplary bed-making and arrangement of bedside tables at his seamen's barracks, Sorokin never distinguished himself in a single area. He never fired a single torpedo; his sub was never grouped with the front-line ships. The only reason he became the commander of a division of nuclear subs under construction was his friendship with Captain First Rank Mikhail Blazhin, the head of the submarine department at the navy's personnel administration. After that, his career rise was guaranteed. The word "nuclear" had a magic aura back in those days, and in the arts of groveling and toadying the man had no equal. But how could Sorokin, a man who never commanded a battle-ready *diesel* sub, let alone a nuclear sub, a man who didn't know the first thing about nuclear power plants—how could *Sorokin* possibly judge the commander and crew of the *K-19*? It's no wonder that Prosyankin, the director of the "Northern Machine-Building Enterprise" (that is, the Severodvinsk Shipyard), called Sorokin a "grasping con man" once he'd had the chance to gauge his abilities.

Sorokin's line was eagerly echoed by our number one slanderer and falsifier, Captain 1st Rank Boris Petrovich Akulov. It was Akulov who falsified the cause of the accident and spread the rumor that the crew should have taken no action at all because there were 16 atmospheres of residual pressure in the primary loop. (To hear him tell it, once the *K-19* was towed in and docked at Andreyeva Bay, he had climbed down into the hold of Compartment Six and gotten a reading of 16 atmospheres on some sort of manometer.) What's more, the pumps were functional and "drawing."

Now, how could any competent individual, particularly an engineer, claim that the primary loop could have contained 16 atmospheres of pressure when there was a hole in it measuring 78.54 square mm?

It was all they needed. There were plenty of people every bit as technically unqualified as these men who seized on this canard and spread it around. And it was exactly what Brigade Commander Captain 1st Rank A. I. Sorokin wanted to see happen. So this disgusting fabrication made the rounds of the nuclear fleet.

Later, of course, scientists would "thoroughly study" our accident, perform some additional calculations and conclude that even if the active zone *had* melted down, no thermal explosion and no meltdown of the reactor pressure vessel would have occurred. But what about Chernobyl? Chernobyl actually proved them wrong. Calculations predicted one thing, but reality confirmed the opposite. There *was* an explosion, a hell of an explosion. Summing up his views of nuclear energy, academician Aleksandrov declared: "Understating the dangers is immoral, but then again, exaggerating those dangers, promoting the spread of unverified rumors, fabricating horror stories that feed into people's anxieties—that, too, is immoral.... The dangers exist. But both the scientific community and the public must do everything possible to minimize them. There already exists, in fact, a reactor designed in such a way that the laws of physics themselves would prevent a recurrence of what happened at Chernobyl. But putting such reactors into production will take time."

Writing about Chernobyl in his memoirs, academician Nikolai Dollezhal, the chief designer of our own (K-19's) reactors,
wondered, "What exactly is it that explodes in such cases?
According to one theory (to which I myself subscribe), it is hydrogen, which undergoes chemical transformations in a runaway
reactor. Such an explosion, in my opinion, is what caused the
destruction in the fourth unit at Chernobyl." There had been a
violet glow above the reactor, and during the worst phase of the
accident aboard the K-19 a light blue flame with a violet tinge
had appeared over the reactor lid. The glow was caused by ion-
ization of the hydrogen in the air under the influence of gamma
and beta radiation. At Chernobyl this phenomenon signaled an
imminent explosion. Why then hadn't academician Dollezhal
analyzed this fact over the 25 years between the K-19 accident
and Chernobyl? Dollezhal wrote: "Shock and profound pain
were my feelings upon learning of the disaster at Chernobyl.
And it was precisely a disaster, not an 'accident,' as it is occa-
sionally described." Then why wasn't Dollezhal shocked by the
accident aboard the K-19? We had fatalities, too, didn't we?
Could it be that he was reluctant to admit his own mistakes?

The authorities had good reason to prohibit telling submariners why the K-19 accident occurred and why its effects
were so devastating: There were no fail-safe procedures for
the reactor in the event of a seal failure—or rupture—in the
primary cooling loop, and the responsibility for this rests
with the chief designer.

★ ★ ★

FOR CAPTAIN ZATEYEV, THE disappointment and sorrow caused
by the large number of deaths and serious injuries to his officers

and crew were to plague him for the rest of his life. Throughout the following months he became more and more disenchanted with the navy's handling of nuclear-power safety and attempted to use the knowledge he gained from his experiences aboard the K-19 to help rectify many problems.

Zateyev spent the remaining years of his naval career trying in vain to improve the lot of the sailors serving in nuclear submarines. He departed the active navy and entered the naval reserve in 1978.

CHAPTER EIGHT

THE WARNINGS FROM Zateyev and others like him would be ignored. The Soviets finally had nuclear-powered submarines they could use to combat the United States, and they would deploy them. As these poorly designed and constructed boats were fitted with ever developing and inadequately tested technology, they would sink on a frighteningly regular basis.

From 1958 to 1968, the Soviet Navy lost more than seven submarines and 200 men, and more than 400 crewmen were gravely irradiated. During these hurry-up years of Soviet naval expansion, serious radiation casualties were usually spirited away to isolated hospital wards, where their symptoms were disguised as nervous disorders. Many were classified as suffering from "trauma caused by stress." Scores more died of radiation poisoning, their remains hidden in unmarked graves. Many are still unaccounted for. The Supreme Soviet, the Soviet legislature which normally rubber-stamped Party Central Committee decrees into law, made it unlawful for medical authorities to enter "radiation poisoning" as cause of death on official death certificates.

★ ★ ★

THE JULY 1961 accident only marked the beginning of troubles that would continue to beset *K-19*: the near catastrophe aboard the first Soviet nuclear-powered strategic submarine was a precursor of other, darker things to come.

Following her return to Polyarny under tow in July 1961, the *K-19* was moved to the shipyard in Severodvinsk, where she underwent an extended decontamination, extensive repairs, and modifications to her propulsion plant. The entire reactor room, Compartment Six, was cut out of the submarine hull and replaced with an entirely new power plant. In January 1964 the *K-19* returned to service, undertaking routine strategic patrols in the North Atlantic. The *K-19* conducted strategic deterrent patrols until December 1968, when she entered the shipyard for scheduled conversion of her main missile batteries. The conversion enabled the *K-19* to launch her ballistic missiles while submerged.

On November 15, 1969, while submerged, the *K-19* collided with the American submarine U.S.S. *Gato,* which was conducting surveillance of the submarine in the Barents Sea. *K-19* sustained only minor damage to her bow from the collision, and from October 1970 through April 1974 the submarine conducted five missile patrols in the Atlantic.

While returning from a patrol at a depth of 450 feet on February 24, 1972, the unlucky submarine suffered a major fire in the after machinery of Compartment Nine. A leaking high-pressure hydraulic seal spilled fluid onto a hot filter that ignited a major fire that burned out of control, killing 28 crewmen before the remaining crew could be evacuated forward to Compartment Eight. Fires then erupted in Compartments Five and Eight. While fighting the fire and trying desperately to drive the submarine to the surface, 12 men were trapped in the after torpedo room, Compartment Ten.

The commanding officer, Captain Second Rank Viktor Kulibaba, brought the submarine to the surface and sent an emergency assistance signal. While rescue forces raced to the scene, a winter storm began to blow, with winds of more than one hundred miles per hour, a force eight gale. Efforts by a Soviet ocean tug to take the stricken *K-19* under tow failed due to the high seas. The missile cruiser *Vice Admiral Drozd*, sent to assist from the Northern Fleet, managed to evacuate most of the surviving crew, leaving an 18-man damage-control party aboard in Compartment Three, plus the 12 men still trapped inside the after part of the hull. The storm raged for three weeks while the men inside Compartment Ten, in complete darkness, survived on tinned rations and water collected with rags from condensation on the hull while Compartment Nine still smoldered next door.

When the seas finally abated, rescuers found the 12 men alive but partially blinded and suffering from extreme exposure and malnutrition. The *K-19* was towed back to base, repaired, and restored to the fleet. In 1976 the *K-19's* missile systems were again upgraded, and she was converted into a Project 658 C-type missile submarine with longer-range missiles. Shortly following this latest conversion, and while in port, she suffered an oxygen explosion and fire in her reactor compartment. She was taken back to the shipyard and reconfigured as a special communications platform, re-named the *KS-19* and served until 1988, when another fire struck her Second Compartment.

KS-19 was finally taken from active service in 1990 and decommissioned in 1991. Zateyev attended a reunion of former *K-19* crewmen at the decommissioning ceremony where the unlucky submarine's flag was lowered and she was placed in the inactive fleet. Portions of Zateyev's memoir describing the 1961 reactor accident were quoted at the ceremony. The submarine, nicknamed "Hiroshima," is still moored alongside a deserted pier in Shkval shipyard in Polyarny.

★ ★ ★

AT LEAST SHE STAYED afloat. That could not be said for a number of other Soviet submarines, which would receive burials in the seas. One such accident happened to another of this first wave of new boats.

Nuclear submarine pioneer Captain Leonid Ossipenko's celebrated first Soviet atomic-powered attack submarine, launched in 1957, was the *K-3*. This boat, also named *Leninsky Komsomol,* was the first Soviet submarine to navigate under the Arctic ice, surfacing at the North Pole on July 17, 1962. For that achievement Ossipenko and his second-in-command, Lev Zhiltsev, were awarded the order of Hero of the Soviet Union by Nikita Khrushchev. During the epic cruise to the pole a leak in a reactor steam generator mortally irradiated a dozen *K-3* crewman, an incident that was quietly suppressed. Four years later, the same submarine lost 39 crewmen in a fire, limped back to port, and was decommissioned. It was dumped in the Barents Sea near Novaya Zemlya in an expanding graveyard of failed Soviet atomic projects.

The record of the first Soviet liquid-metal-cooled reactor was a fiasco. The Soviets built the *K-27*, almost identical to a Project *Kit* attack submarine, with the new experimental reactor. Among other things, liquid-metal-cooled reactors offer the promise of greater power from a smaller reactor, and so were experimented with by both the Soviets and the Americans. The Soviet experience was considerably worse than what the U.S. Navy suffered with a similar engineering plant in the U.S.S. *Seawolf*. This American prototype was equipped with a sodium-cooled reactor. The system proved difficult to operate, and large amounts of leaking sodium coolant, which solidified, had to be shoveled gingerly from the reactor compartment by concerned crewmen. This reactor was eventually replaced by a pressurized-water reactor.

The *K-27* sustained a coolant freeze (when the lead-bismuth liquid metal coolant solidified) on her maiden voyage to mid-Atlantic latitudes in 1964. The next year, she suffered a series of six major casualties. Finally, in May 1968, the *K-27* experienced a severe radiological accident, following a liquid coolant freeze. Nine crewmen were killed. *K-27* was then towed to Novaya Zemlya and abandoned. Ffteen years later, in 1981, the submarine was scuttled in 60 meters of water with her damaged reactors still aboard. The scuttling was carried out despite protests and warnings by senior nuclear engineers who were gravely concerned about safeguarding the partially spent reactor fuel that remained inside the damaged reactor casing.

Misfortune struck the Soviet prototype atomic surface ships as well as their submarines. The world's first nuclear-powered icebreaker, the much heralded *Lenin*, built in the late 1950s, suffered severe damage to most of the fuel element in one of her three reactors, which had been left without cooling through operator error. The accident, which reportedly killed at least 30 crewmen late in 1965, required that 95 percent of the reactor fuel be removed and replaced. In a second accident in 1967 during a refueling, another of her three reactors was gutted and discarded near Novaya Zemlya. Portions of the discarded equipment are still highly contaminated—including three reactors, a circulating pump with contaminated primary reactor-cooling piping, and numerous barrels of spent nuclear fuel. These lie scattered 150 feet below the surface of the Kara Gulf at the Tsivolka Inlet, excreting poisonous nuclear contamination into the Barents Sea.

★ ★ ★

THE NAME OF THE chief engineer of the first nuclear submarine, Nikolai Mormul, became well known in the long journey of Soviet submarine misfortune. Following the disasters aboard icebreaker *Lenin* and submarines *K-3*, *K-8* and *K-19*, and then the *K-27*, resulting in the loss of more than 250 navy men, nuclear engineer Mormul became an open critic of Soviet submarine safety. He began his futile attempts to prevent more accidents by submitting detailed procedures for operating and improving submarine power plants to the Main Navy Engineering Directorate in Moscow. He immediately fell into disfavor with the naval high command for steadfastly refusing to stop his attempts to rewrite nuclear engineering procedure. Admiral of the Fleet Sergei Gorshkov ordered Mormul cashiered for lack of patriotic zeal and for attempting to expose the sorry plight of the early Soviet submarine force. Mormul's real crime, however, was daring to advocate improved engineering safety.

In 1986, shortly after the Chernobyl accident, while still in disfavor, Mormul sent General Secretary Mikhail Gorbachev a written procedure to correct deficiencies in the woefully flawed nuclear power plants throughout Russia. Again his expertise was ignored, and he was labeled a nuisance.

Mormul was finally exonerated by Gorbachev in 1987 during a mass pardon of political dissidents. He was promoted to Kontr Admiral and returned to the Northern Fleet as a senior engineer. Mormul later wrote a book exposing the hidden past of the Soviet submarine force and the deplorable record of nuclear dumping at sea. The book was finally published in Russia in 1996, after being suppressed by security censors since its completion in 1992.

The bright Soviet promise of ships that would patrol endlessly, reaching every corner of the globe, hid a dark underside. Men were dying in this grand experiment. The Americans didn't have to fire a shot. The Russians were willing to kill their own.

A GOLF IS LOST AND FOUND

CHAPTER NINE

THE COLD WAR, THOUGH it contained few instances of open warfare between the Soviet Union and NATO forces, was still a war, and nowhere was this more true then in the ocean. For three decades American and Soviet submarines patrolled the seas—and often encountered each other. Here the glaring technological disparities between the two fleets came to a head.

One of the most remarkable incidents of the undersea war was the loss of a Soviet submarine with all hands that occurred on March 8, 1968, when a Soviet Project 629M diesel-powered ballistic missile submarine disappeared in the northern Pacific. The cause of sinking of the submarine, which Soviets called *K-129*, has never been determined.

The ill-fated *K-129* had been assigned to the Pacific Fleet Submarine Division 22. Kontr Admiral Victor A. Dygalo, the division's former commander, related the story in 1995. Dygalo, longtime assistant editor of the Soviet Navy digest *Morskoi Sbornik*, provided his personal account of the entire story neatly printed in his own hand. To this day, the kindly and deeply religious former submariner believes the United States Navy caused the disappearance of the submarine and the deaths of all 97 crewmen aboard.

Dygalo's account alleges that *K-129* was proceeding on a covert transit to a mid-Pacific patrol station, snorkeling intermittently, when she was intercepted and trailed by an American nuclear attack submarine. While tracking the Soviet, the American sub maneuvered actively and passed beneath the target at critically short distances to study and photograph the hull. According to Dygalo, a collision occurred when the Soviet turned suddenly, exposing her broad side. The maneuver was not immediately noticed by the trailing American, and the upper portion of her sail struck the bottom of the Soviet submarine's Central Command Post while at a depth of 150 feet. *K-129* went down after struggling for nearly 30 minutes and surfacing briefly. As she sank, U.S. passive sonar devices recorded the progressive popping sounds of her compartments collapsing in the tremendous pressure as the hull fell three miles to the bottom.

Dygalo maintains that U.S. Pacific Fleet command representatives denied a collision took place, claiming that the crushing sounds of the sinking Soviet submarine were heard and pinpointed by the U.S. undersea passive acoustic listening arrays, called the Sound Surveillance System (SOSUS)—explaining the U.S. knowledge of the precise location of the sinking.

Admiral Dygalo was convinced from the beginning that the American attack submarine began to trail *K-129* during the latter's reconnaissance mission off the Pearl Harbor submarine base in Hawaii. The sequence of her last communications and the fact that the Golf-class boat was found on the seabed with the bottom of her hull torn open prove, according to Dygalo, that she was involved in an underwater collision with another submarine.

According to the admiral, as soon as the submarine failed to communicate during two designated reporting sessions, she was declared missing. As the division commander, Dygalo was responsible for reporting the loss to the Pacific Fleet Commander in Chief, Admiral Ivan Amelko, who was absent from headquarters aboard cruiser *Dmitry Pozharsky.*

Dygalo explained further that the Soviets suspected that American units had detected *K-129* and tracked her until March 8. "We had one signal from her that she was being pursued by American ASW forces; we presume both air and submarine. There was no doubt an incident with those forces accounted for her failure to send a scheduled signal. We feared then that the submarine had been lost."

Admiral Amelko retained his fleet command after the loss, but he ordered that after *K-129,* no more Soviet diesel-electric submarines conduct surveillance assignments against Pearl Harbor. It was too risky for a diesel to recharge batteries so close to the U.S. antisubmarine defenses.

The search for *K-129* continued fruitlessly for several months while the U.S. Pacific Command quietly guarded their knowledge of the *K-129's* exact position. If the position of the lost Golf was known by other means, possibly by the unit that caused her sinking, the United States Navy still guards the information as classified. While fragments of the records about the CIA-sponsored recovery of that submarine have been released to the public, the U.S. Navy, specifically the submarine force, will not release their accounts of the contact and pursuit of the *K-129* by antisubmarine warfare (ASW) forces of the Pacific Fleet.

The U.S. Navy apparently knew of the exact location of the sinking and, after a pause, dispatched forces to search for the wreck. An oceanographic research ship named U.S.N.S. *Mizar* and a specially configured deep-sea reconnaissance submarine called U.S.S. *Halibut* were dispatched to locate and survey the sunken Soviet sub. U.S.S. *Halibut SSGN* 587 was a one-off nuclear submarine originally configured to carry the Regulus I surface-launched cruise missile with an 80-mile range. She was extensively reconfigured in 1965 as a deep-sea reconnaissance and retrieval submarine, and re-designated as *SSN-587*. *Halibut* had huge compartments that housed spools of cable for deploying observation equipment miles below the ocean surface.

Finding the lost Soviet submarine on the bottom four months after she sank, *Halibut* reconnoitered the wreck, obtained photographs, and retrieved some items from the hull—an incredible accomplishment in 1968. The *Halibut's* actions were kept under wraps until her role was exposed in *The New York Times* in February 1994. The U.S. Navy has never declassified or released the photos of the Golf on the bottom. One of the photos was alleged to be the skeletal remains of a Soviet sailor, wearing a life jacket and foul-weather gear, lying on the ocean floor. According to some, this photo indicated that whatever caused her sinking occurred while the submarine was on the surface. Admiral Dygalo pointed out, however, that if the photo was authentic, it would indicate that the Golf had clawed her way to the surface while struggling to remain afloat before finally sinking. The fact that the submarine's snorkel and periscopes were in the stowed position while the submarine remains lay on the bottom is, in Dygalo's mind, sufficient proof that whatever caused the sinking occurred while she was submerged, and if she had reached the surface, she had done so with her periscopes stowed, probably due to damage incurred.

After studying the site and the exterior condition of the submarine's remains, the CIA planned a salvage operation. A deep-sea mining vessel called *Glomar Explorer*, built and operated by the CIA under cover of the Summa Corporation, returned to the site in 1974 and retrieved portions of the submarine. The remarkable salvage operation was leaked to the Western press during its progress but continued until completion despite the arrival of several Soviet ships that watched intently at close range but did not interfere.

The recovery ship *Glomar Explorer* was built to resemble an underwater mining platform. It lowered a clawlike device on the end of a three-mile pipe string and grasped the largest hull section of the submarine and began hoisting it to the surface. The physics of the feat can best be described as trying to remove a hat from a man's head by dangling a hook on a string from the top of the Empire State Building.

As the wreck neared the surface, its great weight caused one section to break free and fall back to the depths while the remainder was placed into a barge inside the *Glomar Explorer's* well deck. Roughly the forward third of the submarine's hull was retrieved, which did not include the missile silos in the sail. After carefully preparing the wreck for inspection, submarine construction experts, naval intelligence, and forensic inspectors entered the hull and searched through the remains of the twisted wreck. The searchers recovered some valuable communications equipment and portions of the nuclear warheads from two torpedoes.

The most startling discovery was the crude construction of the hull and the signs of shoddy maintenance. Engineers found that the submarine's hull plates had irregular thicknesses and were of inconsistent manufacture. Internal hatches did not fit snugly and were obviously not watertight. Some sections of the hull were supported by wooden shoring where poor-quality welding had failed. High pressure air and hydraulic piping showed signs of excessive leakage. In some sections engineers found scores of moveable lead weights that were apparently used to trim the boat by hand when at sea. These discoveries astounded the American submarine analysts and were unlike the highly sophisticated weapons technology found in the torpedoes and parts of missiles recovered during earlier operations. The inside of the hull and the human remains showed traces of contamination from plutonium spilled from the torpedo warheads, which had been twisted by the extreme pressure of the three-mile depth.

Remains of what appeared to be six sailors were gathered, carefully placed in a container, and buried at sea. The burial was conducted with full military honors and videotaped as evidence that the process had been carried out with dignity.

The initial disclosures of the *K-129's* sinking in the Russian press in 1989 provided the impetus to start a dialog between the Soviet and American Navies to resolve scores of other submarine accidents. Soviet interest focused on the annual review of the U.S.- Soviet Incidents at Sea Prevention accord—an agreement between the two navies signed in 1972 to prevent the growing number of dangerous incidents between ships and aircraft of both sides. The Soviet Navy regularly submitted a request at these annual meetings to include submarine operations under the agreement; but the U.S. Navy still refuses to agree to that proposal. American officers insisted the 1972 agreement applied only to surface ships and aircraft, claiming that placing restrictions of any kind on U.S. submarines would violate their traditional autonomy of operations.

An attempt to acquire confirmation of the *K-129* salvage from the U.S. government in 1975 resulted in limited success when Secretary of State Henry Kissinger passed the names of three of the deceased seamen who had been identified to Soviet Ambassador Anatoli Dobrynin. That was the last information offered by the United States government regarding the incident before the Soviet Union collapsed in 1991. The following year, during initial sparring for joint cooperation, the CIA and the former KGB began to meet on a limited basis. During one of the early meetings, CIA officials offered the Russians some documentary evidence including the videotape showing the burial at sea.

American officers have refuted the Russian charge made early on that American nuclear attack submarine U.S.S. *Swordfish* was the U.S. submarine involved—a charge based solely on the latter's reported arrival in the Ship Repair Facility, Yokosuka, Japan, on March 12, 1968, with a badly damaged sail. Retired U.S. Navy Admiral William D. Smith informed Dygalo by letter following a August 31, 1994, meeting of a Joint U.S./Russia Commission examining questions of Cold War and previous war missing, that the allegation of *Swordfish's* involvement was not correct and that *Swordfish* was nowhere near the Golf on March 8, 1968. The joint commission, headed by General Volkogonov and Ambassador Malcomb Toon, informed the Russians that no U.S. submarines on March 8, 1968, had been within 300 nautical miles of the site where the *K-129* was found.

Despite the Soviet readiness to claim that their submarine losses were due to collisions with American or other Western submarines, there is no doubt that the vast majority of Soviet submarine casualties during the Cold War were self-inflicted. The years following 1968 would see continued losses, often of entire submarines sinking to the bottom of the sea. There they still lie today, their nuclear reactors rotting and leaking their deadly wastes.

SUNKEN POISON

==========

CHAPTER TEN

THE FIRST NUCLEAR-POWERED sub-
marine to be completely lost at sea
was the Project 627 *Kit K-8*. This unit
was returning from a Mediterranean Sea
patrol following the worldwide Soviet
Navy exercise called Okean 1970 when
fires erupted simultaneously in Compartments Three and
Eight while the submarine was submerged off the Bay of Bis-
cay in April 1970. When the fires burned out of control, the
commanding officer ordered the submarine abandoned except
for a small crew of engineers, who remained aboard to continue to fight the fire. As the fire continued to smolder,
Moscow Naval Headquarters ordered the commanding officer to reboard the submarine and to attempt to save it. Fifty-
two men returned aboard in a gallant attempt to save the boat,
but *K-8* suddenly sank, taking all to the bottom. The cause
of the fire is still unknown.

Unfortunately, *K-8* was only the first casualty. According to the official Yablokov Report, a survey commissioned by the Boris Yeltsin government of the Russian Federation in 1992, eight Russian submarines lie at the bottom of the Atlantic, Barents, and Pacific, along with eighteen reactors in various states of damage—six still containing partially spent nuclear fuel. This total includes those submarines scuttled with their reactors still aboard. Additionally, more than 46 nuclear warheads are scattered in the world's seabeds—44 of them in 18,000 feet of water 450 miles northeast of Bermuda, where they were lost inside the hull of the world's first nuclear-powered submarine to sink at sea loaded with ballistic missiles—a Project 667 *Navaga* submarine with 16 missiles, each tipped with two nuclear warheads. The Project *Navaga* submarine foundered and sank following an explosion and fire in October 1986 while patrolling off the eastern coast of the United States. The explosion was caused by the unstable liquid missile fuel, which ignited when agitated by a seawater leak. The missile and two attached atomic warheads were blown through the silo hatch and in fragments into the sea, scattering the powderlike warhead plutonium throughout the hull of the submarine. The explosion and resulting fire caused considerable alarm in the United States as the accident occurred just five days prior to the celebrated Reagan-Gorbachev summit meeting in Reykjavik, Iceland.

Two crewmen were killed in the initial blast. Fires quickly broke out in the adjacent missile compartment. Fumes from the missile's burning liquid fuel, which seeped throughout the boat in the form of nitric acid, ate away at hatch gaskets, destroying watertight integrity, and corroded the insulation on electrical wires. Efforts to shut down the two reactors initially failed when all remote reactor controls were lost due to the corrosion of the electric controls. As a last resort to prevent what they thought would be a disastrous nuclear meltdown, two men entered the active reactor compartment and lowered the control rods by hand. An engineer-seaman by the name of Sergei Preminin heroically shut down one reactor, carried his unconscious reactor officer to safety, then returned to shut down the remaining reactor. He died inside the reactor compartment.

The fumes from the burning missile fuel caused severe nitric acid burns in the lungs of many crewmen. As the crew fought for more than 12 hours to save the boat, she began gradually to take on water, settling by the bow. The commanding officer, Captain Second Rank Igor Britanov, evacuated his crew to waiting Soviet merchant ships, keeping only a damage-control party aboard. Captain Britanov then refused Moscow's orders to reboard the sinking ship, and finally ordered all his men off the foundering boat, while remaining aboard himself, alone, until the very last moment. In a dramatic scene, with the submarine sinking bow first in the dark Atlantic night, Captain Britanov left his stricken boat in a rubber life raft and was rescued by his crewmen, who were searching the waters in motor launches from the merchant ships.

Unstable liquid missile and torpedo fuel caused numerous accidents in the Soviet fleet, including the super-submarine *Kursk*, lost in August 2000. In a similar case, another Project *Navaga* submarine, with improved-range missiles but still liquid-fueled, intentionally opened one missile silo door and ejected a ballistic missile, complete with atomic warhead, into the Pacific Ocean to preclude an onboard explosion. Frantic efforts by the navy successfully retrieved the errant warhead a few days later.

One of the most chilling accidents occurred in April 1989 aboard the *Komsomolets*, *K-287*, a revolutionary titanium-hulled, nuclear-powered submarine. This boat was capable of diving to more than 3,000 feet and was designed with the latest in Soviet nuclear submarine technology.

The submarine caught fire in the northern Norwegian Sea while on an Atlantic patrol. The fire, which was started by hydraulic fluid in the rudder steering mechanism, was never completely contained. It spread quickly to five additional compartments when electrical surges ignited scores of remote-control instruments. The crew was unable to contain the fire, particularly after a high-pressure air line ruptured and fanned the fires into blowtorch intensity. The extreme temperatures caused paint on equipment and inside the hull to flash, and protective rubber masks melted on the crewmen's faces. Many of the crew were poisoned when pressure in one burning space forced carbon monoxide into the ship-wide emergency breathing system—which many of the firefighters had plugged into with flexible breathing hoses.

Within a few minutes the control room watch drove the stricken submarine to the surface from a depth of 500 feet. While the ship wallowed helplessly on the surface as the crew fought the fires, her oxygen and lubricating oil tanks suddenly exploded, rupturing the pressure hull and causing progressive flooding. The boat settled slowly at first and then rapidly sank stern first before rescuers arrived on the scene. Most of the crew of *Komsomolets* had abandoned ship into the arctic waters without survival equipment while she was still on the surface.

The commanding officer, Captain Second Rank Yevgeny Vanin, remained in the submarine in a valiant effort to save those still aboard as she sank stern first to the bottom. Most of the 42 crewmen lost in the disaster succumbed to exposure in the near-freezing seawater.

The nuclear-powered cruiser *Kirov* was the first navy ship to arrive on the scene of the *Komsomolets* sinking. It took aboard some of the survivors pulled from the frigid waters. Two of those rescued died even after receiving clean bills of health from the cruiser's medical officer. The two subsequently ate a large meal and succumbed suddenly after lighting and inhaling deeply on cigarettes. According to the doctor, they had suffered from extreme smoke inhalation that had not been diagnosed. Other survivors told of inflatable life rafts sinking directly when tossed from rescue aircraft and survival clothing that leaked, exposing the sailors to the frigid waters.

Even more horrible was the malfunctioning of the submarine's integral emergency rescue chamber. According to the cruiser's medical officer, who treated the sole survivor of the five who surfaced from the depths in that steel cell, it was a terrifying experience:

> *The captain, Yevgeny Vanin, remained aboard his sub when it suddenly began to sink. Vanin was a brave man. When all others were trying to save themselves, he tried to save those still inside the sub by putting them into the rescue chamber — even as the sub went down like a rock. Warrant Officer Slyusarenko was the only one of the five to come out of the chamber alive.*
>
> *Slyusarenko told me how Captain Vanin found four others still aboard and helped them, on their hands and knees, to enter the rescue chamber. Mind you, the sub wasn't sinking on an even keel. They had to move uphill, crawling hand over hand up the passageways, over hatch coamings, opening doors above their heads.*
>
> *Another officer, Yudin, and Warrant Officer Chernikov closed the bottom access hatch after climbing inside the sphere. The cap-*

tain told Yudin to prepare to detach the capsule from the sub's hull. Just before attempting to release the capsule from the submarine, those inside heard a frantic clanging on the bottom hatch. One more crewman, apparently the submarine's engineer, was trying to enter the sealed rescue sphere. Those inside the chamber tried to reopen the lower hatch but couldn't. The sphere already had several meters of water covering the bottom hatch, which made it virtually unmovable.

To the horror of the men inside the sphere, it kept plunging deeper. They couldn't detach from the submarine hull. Yudin tried the release lever again, but nothing happened. "How does it work?" Yudin yelled.

"Read the instructions," the captain answered. They never once practiced with the rescue chamber. They were forced to read the instructions as they sank! Someone, by sheer unusual forethought, had posted written instructions next to the release mechanism. Can you imagine? Sinking in a burning submarine, and poor Yudin had to stop and read the instructions?

Still worse, the knocking continued as the submarine's compartments popped one by one with a sickening crunch. They plunged past their crush depth of 3,000 feet — the depth meter in the sphere broke at just 1,200 feet.

According to Slyusarenko, Yudin was calmly reading the posted list of steps to take when they crashed on the sea bottom and the rescue chamber detached itself and began to float to the surface. Slyusarenko even felt the hull of the compartment collapse next to the sphere.

After finally separating from the submarine hull, the rescue chamber soared quickly to the surface. But that didn't save the five inside. No, even though the sphere was designed to compensate for the pressure changes, it shot to the surface too quickly, killing four of the five men inside with baro-trauma — the bends. Their bodies were ejected like rag dolls through the small hatch in the chamber, which blew open on the surface, venting the pressurized chamber. The capsule filled with water and sank immediately. All died except for Slyusarenko; he was squirted through the hatch when it popped open. He was nearly frozen and had broken limbs and a smashed skull when I got him in here. It was a crime, the lack of training.

The loss of the *Komsomolets* became a celebrated indictment of faulty Soviet submarine design and safety measures. The investigation following the disaster disclosed that the crew of that submarine had never drilled with their modern, sophisticated, automatically releasing life rafts, the escape chamber, or even in basic damage and casualty control. Automatically released signal transmitters, designed to float free from a sinking submarine, rise to the surface, and transmit compressed radio-frequency distress signals via satellite had been tack-welded to the hull by crewmen to ensure against their loss. The deplorable details of the failures in the training of the *Komsomolets* crew are contained in the book *Loss of the Komsomolets, Arguments of the Constructor,* written by one of the original constructors of the project, Dmitry Romanov, who writes:

On October 29, 1955, the battleship Novorossysk *sank at her moorings at her Black Sea base due to an external explosion, with the loss of more than 600 men. The governmental commission for investigating the causes for the loss of the battleship determined that the central structure of the*

navy was ultimately responsible because of insufficient atten-
tion to detail and that responsible cadres were guilty of not
sufficiently training the ship's company for combat readiness
and casualty control and the lack of documentary instruction
in damage control. Thirty-three years later tragedy occurred
aboard submarine Komsomolets *for exactly the same rea-*
sons. A ship sinks, people are lost, and the central structure
of the navy continues as if nothing happened.

More than a mile under the northern Norwegian Sea, Russians installed nine seals to the bow of *Komsomolets* to contain the spread of plutonium leaking from two torpedo warheads. According to the expedition leader, Dr. Sagalevitch, the nine holes in the bow were covered by seals made of rubber and titanium. Six of the holes were for torpedo tubes and three were fractures caused by the sinking.

The Russians abandoned a plan to raise the entire hull as too risky. They were so concerned about the condition of the *Komsomolets* wreck in the Norwegian Sea that they turned to the West for assistance in solving the threat of nuclear effluents escaping. As a result of a joint Russian, American, and European study of the site, the Russians erected a concrete tomb around the shattered hull to contain the 26 pounds of plutonium still present in two nuclear-tipped torpedoes, which were found to be corroding at an alarming rate. The area where the submarine rests is among the most biologically productive in the world's oceans. Even the smallest amounts of radionuclides along the food chain from seawater to plankton to fish could result in grave environmental, economic, and political consequences.

As more accounts of accidents and near-disasters emerged from the former Soviet Union, the chilling facts exposed the narrow gap which existed in the Soviet armed forces between safety and sheer cataclysm. Other versions of the naval tragedies have appeared since then. Most are fragmentary, and they give little more details than presented here of past nuclear accidents, and few fully document the appalling history of Soviet nuclear-waste dumping. Accounts of the accidents and losses are still guarded by the Russian Navy as sensitive. The concern today by international environmental organizations has resulted in more data being squeezed from official records, but cooperation by Russian citizens is rare. The two former naval officers who did help to gather material on past accidents and data regarding the wanton dumping of contaminated solid and liquid nuclear waste were arrested and tried for divulging state secrets. The imprint of the repressive hand of the former regime still casts a shadow over those in possession of data that might further expose the secrets of past nuclear misfortune and help define what needs to be done to reduce the risk of further damage to the environment.

ATOMIC GRAVEYARD

CHAPTER ELEVEN

**T**HE OPENNESS OF THE Gorbachev era had a profound impact on the Soviet Navy. For years the West had suspected that the Soviet Union was concealing its fleet's marginal effectiveness, and those suspicions were now being proved correct. In Moscow, precise information about the fleet's appalling safety conditions, especially aboard nuclear-powered ships, began to percolate to the surface, confirming what had been surmised based on earlier fragmentary intelligence reports and accounts leaked during widening contacts between Western diplomats and Soviet citizens.

More ominous than the gruesome accounts of the individual naval disasters suffered at sea are the revelations of how many nuclear reactors and atomic weapons are scattered in various states of decay on the seafloor. The alarming accounts, which began to surface after 1991, confirm the number and locations of wrecked nuclear reactors and lost atomic warheads lying on the ocean floor, the remains of 40 years of hidden Soviet submarine misfortune. In the Kara Sea dumping area alone, near Novaya Zemlya in the Barents Sea—the largest Soviet nuclear graveyard—more than 3.5 million curies of nuclear waste already on the seabed were disclosed in 1992. That is the equivalent of one-tenth of the radiological contamination leaked to the atmosphere during the Chernobyl incident. The residue exists in the form of eight scuttled submarine hulls, sixteen discarded reactors—six with fuel still inside—and 9,000 additional tons of discarded fuel assemblies and liquid nuclear waste, all in water no deeper than 150 feet.

Between the late 1950s and 1993, the normal procedure for the Russian Navy was to dump liquid and solid radioactive waste and spent nuclear fuel at sea in designated sites in the Barents and Pacific. Testimony by Nikolai Mormul and other witnesses in the disposal business claim that vast quantities of nuclear waste were disposed during the Soviet years without any records, at night in areas not authorized for dumping in the Barents Sea in the north and in the Sea of Japan off Pacific Fleet ports. An accurate accounting of early nuclear-waste disposal is impossible.

Unauthorized, secret dumping of radioactive waste at sea was the product of the so called "stagnation period"—1964 to 1983—in Soviet history, when senior naval and shipyard personnel avoided accepting responsibility for their actions for fear of repercussions.

Following the disclosures of the disastrous Soviet Navy safety record, and feeling increasing international pressure to end nuclear dumping at sea, Russian President Boris Yeltsin commissioned a team in 1992 to report on nuclear dumping in the areas around the former Soviet naval bases. The study, known by its short name as the Yablokov Report, was released a year later.

For years the official U.S. and Russian Navy response to criticism of dumping nuclear debris has been that the best place to dispose of old reactors and warheads is in deep mud on the seabed, the deeper the better. Yet according to experts at Woods Hole Oceanographic Institution, this theory is valid only if the reactor container or missile casings are well sealed and intact. How long such containers can remain unchanged on the seabed is an unanswered question.

Inactive nuclear-powered ships that contain fueled reactors require continuous electrical power to keep cooling liquids circulating until de-fueled. Reactor core fuel elements require a continuous flow of cooling water to remove accumulating heat, or a reactor could overheat and cause an explosion when exposed to seawater. That means continuous electrical power is required to run pumps for circulating seawater to remove heat from steam generators through which secondary coolant passes, removing heat from primary coolant. Therefore, all nuclear submarines that await dismantling require power and manning by engineers to assure safety.

There are three basic ways to dispose of used reactors when decommissioning nuclear-powered ships: dumping at sea, long-term storage on land, and the complete disposal by burial in a deep repository. All three options can be preceded by a prolonged period of storage afloat inside sealed reactor compartments, which have been cut out of the ship. During the storage phase the reactor must be sealed in a container that is sufficiently corrosion resistant and secure for the period of storage. All of the disposal choices expose involved workers to radiation, both as they are preparing the submarine hull or the isolated compartment for disposal and over the long term from radioactivity at the disposal site.

The Soviet Navy dumped reactor compartments directly into the ocean from ships and submarines whose reactors had been damaged in accidents, including those from the icebreaker *Lenin* and submarines *K-3*, *K-11*, *K-19,* and *K-27*. Deep-sea dumping is by far the least costly, and has the least risk of causing exposure during the dumping process, although the longer-term implications for the global population could be significant if large numbers of reactors are dumped. The Soviet Navy routinely dumped poorly prepared, accident-damaged reactors containing fuel assemblies in shallow waters in the Kara Sea and the Sea of Japan. Although some precautions were taken to prevent seepage from dumped reactors, Russian authorities acknowledge their uncertainty in assessing the potential for serious contamination in the years to come. U.S. Navy experts claim the best place for a damaged reactor is at the bottom of the sea, the deeper the better. The threat posed by nuclear weapons lost in the sea is a much different issue. Plutonium from an atomic warhead, although heavy enough to sink into the seabed, has the potential for remaining a threat to sea life and the food chain for its entire half life, or decay period, which is estimated as 200,000 years, a grim prospect at best.

Dumping of naval reactors should not be considered in isolation, but in conjunction with the very large inventories of radioactive waste, both civilian and military, that were dumped by the Soviet Union. Large amounts of low- and intermediate-level radioactive waste have been routinely disposed in the sea at more than 50 sites in the North Atlantic and Pacific Oceans. Sea dumping, which started in 1946, was halted only by international moratorium in 1982. The acknowledged dumping of marine reactor assemblies and irradiated equipment by the Soviet Union surpassed that dumped by all other nations combined.

The Kara Sea dumping was made in continental shelf waters off Novaya Zemlya at depths of between 20 and 150 meters, compared to the organized and declared dumping of the West, which all took place in deep-ocean waters.

Neither the former Soviet Union authorities nor the current Russian Federation government have commented further on radioactive-waste dumping since the release of the Yablokov Report in 1993. Past requests for specific information by the International Atomic Energy Agency have gone unanswered. A survey vessel charted by a joint Norwegian-Russian marine expedition was refused entry into waters off Novaya Zemlya. Greenpeace ship M/V *Solo* was detained for four weeks when lingering off Novaya Zemlya in October 1992.

What is the reason for the Russian stonewalling? It is now known that major changes in Soviet policy and practices in sea dumping reduced the discharge of radioactive waste from 1983 to 1985. During the 20 years prior to that time the Soviets had dumped a variety of radioactive waste. This waste was hauled and dumped by special radioactive-waste ships operated by the Murmansk shipping company, Atomflot, out of Murmansk, servicing the nuclear-powered submarine bases in the Kola Peninsula and the refit and refueling yards at Severodvinsk near Archangelsk. An estimated 16,000 cubic meters of primary-circuit liquid effluents (the most highly radioactive) were dumped at two locations west of Novaya Zemlya, and 11,350 tons of solids, including three complete reactors (4,650 tons) damaged in the *Lenin* icebreaker accidents of 1965 and 1967, were disposed of in relatively shallow waters to the east of Novaya Zemlya. Excluding the *Lenin* reactors, the liquid and solid waste disposed of during the 20-year period equals 160 complete refuelings of twin reactor submarines at the rate of eight refuelings per year.

This would have sustained a peacetime fleet of 50 to 60 submarines, which corresponds with the average size of the Northern Fleet during this period. In other words, the Northern Fleet routinely dumped radioactivity from its nuclear-powered submarines in the Kara and Barents Sea. One specific report that has been uncovered shows that consignments of irradiated fuel were dumped in the Abrosimov Gulf before 1984. Reactor quench baffles, complete with a hundred melted fuel pins from the later *Lenin* icebreaker accident, were disposed of in the Kara Sea in 1972, and some of this waste is now known to have been dumped covertly by submarines equipped for mine laying.

Upon the dissolution of the Soviet Navy in 1991, Russia inherited the world's largest submarine nuclear fleet of 245 boats and now faces the immense task of decommissioning and then dismantling the aging nuclear boats. By 1995, 126 submarines had been decommissioned. Another 80 were scheduled to be decommissioned by the end of the century. Despite assistance from the U.S. and Japan, under the Cooperative Threat Reduction Program, the progress is woefully behind schedule. As of January 2001, 104 nuclear submarines still await decommissioning and safe disassembly. What is worse, the reprocessing of nuclear waste from these submarines is more than five and a half years behind schedule. The Russian naval nuclear support infrastructure, already in decrepit condition when the U.S.S.R. collapsed in 1991, is now stretched to the limit with inactive submarines, their nuclear fuel still aboard, stacked up and abandoned at bases scattered throughout small bays and inlets in the barren Northern and Pacific Fleet areas.

A report released in 1996 by the Bellona Foundation, a Norwegian-based environmental group that once had offices in Russia before being ejected, details the serious environmental threat that Russian nuclear naval facilities pose to the surrounding regions and indicates that Russia is unable and unwilling to make the necessary expenditures to remedy the situation.

According to the Russian Northern Fleet, Sources of Radioactive Contamination, the disposal of solid and liquid radioactive waste is the major problem plaguing the decommissioning program. One of the more serious threats to safety is the failure to properly maintain the storage facilities for spent nuclear fuel and radioactive waste. According to Admiral Oleg Yerofeev, Commander of the Northern Fleet in 1995, "The problems of storing spent nuclear reactor fuel, radioactive waste, inactive submarines and the lack of servicing for the submarines in active service are a problem not only for the Northern Fleet, but also for the Russian state. Therefore, it would be natural not only for the Fleet to take necessary action, but also for the Ministry of Emergency Situations, Emercom, also to act. If measures are not taken to address the situation today, over a period of time the situation could become critical and lead to an ecological disaster."

Constraints on dismantling inactive nuclear-powered submarines and surface ships include limited shipyard capacity, spent-fuel management and disposal of liquid and solid radioactive waste, storage of separated submarine reactor compartments, and institutional and financial deficiencies. Russia's Pacific Fleet, for example, currently stores 10,000 atomic fuel rods from dismantled submarines aboard two rusting ships in the Sea of Japan and at a storage facility southeast of Vladivostok. The storage ships' hull conditions are so bad they are in danger of sinking alongside their piers. The combined radioactive level aboard these two repository ships is four million curies. Plus, the two ships and the Pacific Fleet land storage facility are already filled to capacity. A program to build a proper barge to treat nuclear waste is also more than five and a half years behind schedule, despite assistance from the U.S. and Japan.

Due to the current overall storage conditions, Russia practically had to cease dismantling nuclear submarines in 1997, and the number scheduled to be retired continues to pile up. Of 300 Russian submarine reactors requiring disposal before the end of the last century, only 97 were disassembled. In an effort to ease the problem, Russia requested Western assistance. The United States has been unwilling to offer more than limited financial help. The U.S. Navy, which has an unblemished record of dismantling shipboard reactors, is understandably reluctant to take on the task of untangling the deplorable nuclear navy situation in Russia. Although some United States, Norwegian, and Japanese assistance has been provided to ease the Russian crisis, the U.S. Navy has resisted spending more until Russia reduces or ends its dwindling submarine construction programs—something that is not likely to happen if the U.S. continues to produce nuclear submarines. This means hundreds of reactors will remain in their fueled condition, inside rusting and abandoned submarines awaiting dismantlement—a chilling prospect.

Worse still is the continuing tendency to suppress this information. Since 1995 Russian security authorities have carried out a major operation to stifle the flow of details concerning the true state of the Russian maritime regions and specifically the hazardous conditions in the former Soviet nuclear fleet areas. A coordinated effort is still under way to block foreign access to information regarding the conditions of nuclear-fuel storage and the conditions of more than 270 reactors aboard inactive submarines and surface ships awaiting dismantlement.

To suppress exposure of information, the Russian Federation government returned to using tactics reminiscent of the Soviet

KGB. On October 5, 1995, for example, Russian Federal Security Bureau agents ransacked the Murmansk office of the environmental organization Bellona. The agents confiscated all the data collected concerning nuclear safety in the Northern Fleet area.

The net was cast wider on February 6, 1996, when Russian Navy Captain First Rank Alexandr Nikitin was arrested. The former nuclear engineer was working with Bellona to compile research for the 1996 report on the nuclear safety conditions in Northern Fleet area. Nikitin was jailed and accused of espionage and high treason against Russia for stealing and selling top-secret material to a foreign agency.

On November 23, 1997, the Federal Security Service arrested another former nuclear submariner, Captain First Rank Grigory Pasko, on suspicion of spying after he returned to Vladivostok from a business trip to Japan. His wife and supporters immediately claimed the charges were spurious and that authorities were hounding Pasko for exposing the navy's mishandling of nuclear materials.

The Pasko case was ominously similar to Nikitin's. Pasko was also accused of high treason, a crime that carries a prison sentence of up to 20 years. Both their trials were linked to Russia's vague laws on state secrets, which were expanded by presidential decree in October 1997. Although information on the environment, by law, cannot be considered a state secret, the new law can be interpreted as including nuclear installations with defense significance because the law provides leeway for broad interpretation by the authorities. Nevertheless, the two cases caused considerable contempt within Russian political circles. The trials for treason both resulted in acquittal, but a retrial of Pasko, which was held in secret, concluded in December 2001 and sentenced him to four years in jail.

This sudden crackdown by the new Russian Federal Security Service also targeted foreign researchers who had, for a time, roamed with relative impunity throughout Russia's formerly closed military areas, collecting data for analysis of nuclear safety and environmental damage caused by outrageous nuclear-waste disposal practices of the Soviet years. Princeton University researcher and former Greenpeace author Joshua Handler narrowly escaped arrest when his Moscow apartment was ransacked by Russian security officers, who confiscated his computer. Handler left Russia quickly at the recommendation of U.S. consular officials. His Russian assistant, however, was arrested and charged with spying for the United States.

In 2000 retired U.S. Navy captain Edmond Pope, in Russia on business for the University of Pennsylvania, was arrested, tried, and convicted of spying because he had made inquiries about the new high-speed *shkval* torpedo-missile that was being tested aboard the *Kursk*. Pope was released after his conviction, but the episode shows how Russia is still held captive by old Soviet thinking.

Since the sinking of the submarine *Kursk* in August 2000 and her salvage the following year, the Russian Navy has entered a new era of public affairs consciousness. This resulted from the scandal surrounding piecemeal disclosure of facts about the accident and the failed efforts to free some crewmen believed to be trapped alive. The loss and the publicity of the accident caused great embarrassment to the Russian Navy leadership. In a situation similar to the loss of the submarine *Komsomolets* in April 1989, which occurred during the years of the new Gorbachev era in the early days of a newly unfettered press, the navy was unable to deal with the free flow of information. Its leadership still lacked a satisfactory public information system that would protect the security of their hardware and concurrently provide adequate care to the families of those lost in the accident. The initial reaction to the loss was to point the finger of blame at a collision with an unidentified Western submarine. The results of the investigation into the causes for the *Kursk* explosion will be crucial to the future of the Russian Navy. The evidence in this case is all contained within the twisted wreckage of the *Kursk* hull, which is contained conveniently inside a Northern Fleet drydock, unlike the other wrecks lying strewn on the bottom of the ocean. There is little to hide in this forensic investigation, which further exposes the glaring truth of the cavalier attitude toward safety practiced in the Russian Navy. The Cold War competition no longer remains as the excuse for the shoddy workmanship or the rushing of submarines with super weapons to sea. The results have been damaging to the senior officers of the Russian military-industrial hierarchy, who are all children of the Soviet system.

★ ★ ★

ON THE WINDSWEPT CONFLUENCE of St. Petersburg's Neva River and Nevka Canal, an old warship rides at a lonely mooring. The cruiser *Aurora* has long been a symbol of the glory of the Russian Navy and the Revolution. Commissioned in 1903, a veteran of the Russo-Japanese War, ignitor of a revolution in 1917, and hero of the siege of Leningrad during the Great Patriotic War, it still proudly flies the Orders of the Red Banner and the October Revolution. The chapters of *Aurora's* history missing from the official Soviet version are the ones revealing a less noble fate. During the deployment of the Russian main battle squadron from the Baltic Sea to the Pacific in 1904, she was struck by rounds from her own sister ships. The following year the fleet was annihilated by the Japanese at the Battle of Tsushima. Few know of *Aurora's* flight from that battle, damaged and listing badly, or of her subsequent internment by the neutral U.S. Navy in Manila Bay until the end of the war. Somehow that part was scratched from the Soviet history books.

Like the history of the cruiser *Aurora*, the history of the Soviet Navy has until recently omitted the many misfortunes suffered in their bid to become a world sea power. Russia today faces the new responsibilities of a democratic society, but is still burdened not only by the remains of the old military-industrial system, but also by the poisonous leftovers of the weapons that were hastily constructed to overpower its adversaries. As Captain Nikolai Zateyev said in his memoir: "A nuclear reactor is decidedly hazardous and has to be safeguarded against accidents and disasters. Making a reactor secure from mishaps is no less complicated than designing it in the first place. The likelihood of various categories of accidents is supposed to be taken into account during the development of any piece of new technology." Unfortunately, Russian navy men still face the threat of ending their lives at the bottom of the sea, in badly constructed ships and submarines. Only after Russia successfully corrects its flawed production system and cleans up its fouled environment can it join the rest of the world in the pursuit of a safe and peaceful life in the new century.

UNCHARTED WATERS: THE GENESIS OF *K-19*
BY KATHRYN BIGELOW,
DIRECTOR OF *K-19: THE WIDOWMAKER*

AFTERWORD

THE TRUE STORY of the *K-19* submarine disaster always looked like natural movie material. It had all the elements:
a built-in "ticking clock" suspense factor
of an impending reactor meltdown aboard
a nuclear submarine, with the potential for
catastrophic global repercussions. At its center was a ferociously
dedicated and charismatic captain whose bold decisions under
pressure saved the boat and its crew.

And above all there were these courageous young men, the
submariners themselves, who knowingly and without hesitation subjected themselves to a lethal dose of radiation,
entering the boat's searingly hot reactor room to repair its
damaged cooling system.

In addition, the story of the *K-19* had one other unique element: the submariners whose heroism we intended to celebrate
were Russian. And from the outset we made it clear that we

intended to depict these men without compromise, as loyal servants of the Soviet State circa 1961, at the height of the Cold War, just one year before the series of events that has become emblematic of the nuclear terrors of that period: The Cuban Missile Crisis.

Obviously moved but with great concern, potential backers of this film would invariably ask: "But who am I in this story? Whom is there in this story that I can identify with?"

I said then exactly what I would say today: That the beauty of this story is that you are they. The excitement and the challenge of this subject for me as a filmmaker has always been to induce an American audience to become the "Other," to identify with the mindset of a group of people who for decades they had regarded as the "Enemy."

It had been clear to me that this was a movie I had to make from the moment in 1996 when I first heard about these unsung Russian heroes who prevented a crisis that, during an already tense geopolitical climate, could have brought us to the brink of war, some of them giving up their lives to do so. National Geographic Television had broadcast a British documentary about these extraordinary events that were shrouded in official silence for almost 30 years.

I initially developed *K-19* under my overall production deal at Working Title Films, and secured the services of screenwriter Louis Nowra (*Map of the Human Heart*). It was Louis who went to Russia in 1997 to meet both the captain and his executive officer who had served on the *K-19* during the disaster, the men whose relationship would eventually become the dramatic spine of our screenplay.

In fact, it was the need for a more sharply focused storyline that led me to turn in 1998 to a new screenwriter, New York playwright Christopher Kyle. I took it for granted that the focus of the story would be the human element, and its strength would not be dependent upon the bells and whistles lavished upon high-tech hardware genre movies. If this story didn't work as a clash between strong-willed men at the bottom of the ocean, trying to make a decision in a catastrophic situation, then it wouldn't work anyway, no matter how many bells and whistles I had. And so I told Chris: "Think of it as just two men alone in a black room, on a bare stage." I was literally thinking that if I couldn't raise the money to tell this story as a film, then I would direct it as a play.

Chris and I worked closely together, and he wrote a wonderful first draft, tight, terse, and sharply focused. And then we flew to Moscow together to conduct an interview of our own with this aging Russian hero, Captain Zateyev—only to learn shortly after we arrived that he had died just two weeks earlier. We were, however, welcome to meet with the captain's widow, and so the next day we drove to the small apartment that she had shared with him an hour and a half outside of Moscow.

Sadly, the building in which this hero of the Soviet Union had lived out his retirement, a Khrushchev-era high-rise made of poured concrete, was in extreme disrepair. The common spaces on the ground floor were thickly decorated with graffiti, with only a clattering, rickety elevator to lift us slowly to the 12th floor.

Antonina Zateyev was a beautiful, petite elderly woman with a face like a heart, her eyes still swollen from having cried for days. Despite the appearance of the rest of the building, her apartment was impeccably clean and orderly. In a position of honor was the armchair that had clearly once been his: The captain's empty chair.

At first, like many of the people we met in Russia, Antonina was understandably suspicious. Like most Americans, ordinary

Russians had been accustomed for years to thinking of anyone connected with the other superpower as a deadly enemy. Just the thought of an American coming into her home, much less a person who was going to turn the life of her late husband into a movie, was a bit much for her to absorb at first. So we began slowly, talking about her life. She and her husband had kept birds, which was a rarity in Russia. One little parakeet was flying around freely in the apartment as we talked, perching on the furniture.

Antonina told us many stories about the captain and about their life together that helped us to form a clearer mental picture of the man: about their deep love and respect for each other, but also about his severe self-discipline and his unyielding sense of duty. "He was like an honored guest in his own home," she said, with a sad smile. And as a parting gesture she removed the black ribbons of mourning from a large framed portrait photograph of the captain and handed it to me. It was an astonishing gift and a profound symbol of the trust she had decided to place in us.

As I was leaving Antonina's apartment, still trying to reassure her that I really did want to capture the reality of this man, she just took me into her arms and started sobbing: "You must tell his story, you must tell his story." From that moment on, all bets were off. Nothing could stop us. Not even the vagaries of Hollywood.

It would not be an exaggeration to say that the riveting portrait of Zateyev that Antonina gave me presided over the entire production process of K-19. It depicted the captain at 50, almost 15 years after the accident, when he had gone through multiple bone marrow transplants to counter the effects of his exposure to radiation, and a period of second-guessing and interrogation that dragged on for weeks, when his actions were minutely scrutinized by a government commission—experiences that would have broken a lesser man. I took his picture with me wherever I went, wherever we happened to be shooting. I was transfixed by the gaze of this man, by the very thought of a person with that level of focus and intensity. Clearly this was a man who had never doubted himself or the soundness of his decisions. A man you would follow into Hell.

My sense of Zateyev, of his confidence and severity, was confirmed and even deepened when Chris Kyle and I went to meet some of his former crewmen. These meetings took place first in Moscow and then in St. Petersburg, where we made an appointment to talk with them in a cavernous old establishment called the Submariner's Club. In its huge entryway only one light out of 18 was working, one pale flickering bulb in the corner as we felt our way up a broad staircase. In a tiny dim room we were confronted by a group of elderly men with wizened faces, who looked up at us with intense curiosity bordering on defiance.

These were proud men. To be a submariner in the Soviet culture of the 1960s was the most coveted of jobs. Your parents became stars in their hometown when you traveled to the Kola Peninsula to ship out on a submarine. But most of them had not been honored or even acknowledged for the sacrifices they had made.

On the contrary, the exact fates of those who died as a result of the disaster were shrouded in secrecy, buried, or disappeared, as if they had never existed. Those who survived returned from that hellish voyage and acted as if nothing had happened. When they went to the hospital once a month for their blood transfusions the official explanation was that they were being treated for a nervous disorder, a humiliation in itself. They had borne the memory in silence for almost four decades. And now here I was, an American, presenting myself as the person who would finally tell this story to the world. Their expression said it all: "Who are you to think you can erase the irrelevance we have been living in?"

And here again, toward the end, there was a moment when a couple of these men, guarded and proud men who were also demonstrative Russians, pulled me aside, welled up, and told me: "You must tell this story."

The submariners helped us to get a sharper sense of the difference between Captain Nikolai Zateyev and his acting Executive Officer Vladimir Yenin (aka Alexei Vostrikov and Mikhail Polenin). They told us that Yenin was your friend, an older brother figure, the one you went drinking with and who would listen to your complaints about niggling regulations. But if you were in a life and death situation, you wanted the stern father, Zateyev, to be making the decisions. You feared him but you trusted him absolutely. They were convinced that it was Zateyev's single-mindedness and sense of purpose that had saved their lives.

With this information to go on Chris and I were able to develop together the dramatic through line of the finished screenplay, which is fiction, based on actual events. In compressing the timeline of events, focusing in on key relationships and a manageable number of crew members as central characters, we decided to change the names of actual people involved so as to not misrepresent, or inadvertently omit, the noble actions of the real heroes of K-19.

We knew that Captain Nikolai Zateyev had been assigned to the boat in part because he was a loyal party man. He understood and could be trusted to ferociously pursue the K-19's urgent mission, the test firing of an unarmed missile in North Atlantic waters. He cared deeply about his men, but like any military leader he accepted the fact that at times his sense of duty would compel him to demand of those men the ultimate sacrifice.

It is important to remember that "show and tell" missions of this sort seemed to be matters of life and death in 1961. The Cold War, after all, was unique in human history in being fought on a mental rather than a physical battlefield. It wasn't enough merely to possess a powerful new weapon. Your armaments would not produce the desired deterrent effect unless your enemy knew that you had them. Thus the *K-19* missile test was designed from the start to be easily detectable by the Americans; it was a way of alerting the U.S. to the fact that their recently deployed Polaris nuclear submarines no longer had the high seas all to themselves.

It always made sense to us to suppose that Zateyev understood and believed in the importance of this mission in a way that no one else on board the *K-19* was equipped to. At a moment of extreme tension during the crisis this difference of understanding led to a dispute (in some accounts bordering on mutiny) between Zateyev and several of his officers. In order to dramatize this conflict more effectively, we extrapolated from what we now knew about Yenin in order to reshape him into a character who embodied the crew's position and could go head-to-head with the captain. In our version, Yenin (who we renamed Polenin) is the boat's former commander, demoted for placing the safety of his men above the fulfillment of a mission whose purpose has not been fully explained to him. In the developing relationship between these men, the film also becomes an exploration of conflicting styles of leadership.

That first trip to Russia was momentous for us. We came home with a deeper commitment than ever to the story we wanted to tell and with the confidence that we now understood how it could best be told. In Hollywood, though, it isn't the periods of all-out effort on a project that are most difficult, but the down times, when your project is becalmed. As so often happens, K-19 was cast adrift for a time, before finding a new permanent berth at Intermedia Films. Now, for the first time, we had a production commitment, and we could begin to talk seriously about casting.

In my mind, Vladimir Yenin, our Polenin, had always been Liam Neeson: physically almost too big for the boat and with an innate generosity and openness in his bearing. And when Intermedia raised the possibility of asking Harrison Ford to play Zateyev, whom we called Alexei Vostrikov, the idea was so perfect that from that moment on it was impossible even to think of anyone else. When Harrison said yes to the project, and to the captain, K-19 was no longer drifting on the often storm-tossed waters of development: It became an inevitability.

We returned to Russia once more before we began to shoot K-19 in 2001, to explore the possibility of staging our dry dock and embarkation sequences at the actual base headquarters of the Russian submarine fleet in Murmansk. In the end this proved to be logistically impossible. Halifax, Nova Scotia, stood in for Murmansk. But the experience of the Kola Peninsula in mid-November, 2000, with the film's Director of Photography, Jeff Cronenweth and First Assistant Director, Steve Danton, influenced our approach to the production strongly.

We were definitely well into the Arctic Circle here, at a time of year when the sun never rose more than 15 degrees above the horizon, a sliver of light that lasted from around 11 a.m. to 2 p.m. every day. Otherwise we lived in a beautiful, mercurial cobalt blue netherworld that didn't feel exactly like either day or night.

One of the strange aspects of this experience has been that while the U.S. military was not willing to offer us help at all, the Russians have always been eager to cooperate. When we traveled to Murmansk, our escort was a highly placed naval official from Moscow. We were asking a lot: No Western civilian had ever in the history of the Soviet Union set foot on this naval base. But our escort understood the implications of what we were planning: An American company was making a movie that was a tribute to a Russian naval hero and was considering shooting some of it on location, at the headquarters of the Russian Northern Fleet. He made it possible for us to see the actual *K-19* and even to stand on her deck.

Early one morning, this wonderful man packed us all into a small bus that clearly had seen better days. Its windows were crusted yellow, as if they were tobacco stained. Every interior surface had a patina of ancient dirt. For almost two hours we rattled along, traversing precariously on hard-packed ice across an endless flat tundra with just a sliver of dim light on the horizon.

And at last we turned down a thin road that sloped toward the shore, and a checkpoint guarded by four achingly young men whose Kalishnikov assault rifles were pointed right at our windows. There was a heated argument between our escort and an officer from the base who was clearly a stickler for tradition, while the guards tensed visibly. Suddenly the gate lifted and we drove through, past a boundary that no Western civilian has ever crossed, into a top secret Russian military installation.

It was an eerie spectacle: Under that dome of unnatural blue we saw a row of docks, one after another, extending as far as the eye could see. Moored at each of these docks were Cold War-era, Soviet diesel and nuclear submarines, five or six deep, their hulls in visible disarray, the exposure taking its toll on the metal.

We went out to the end of one of these docks and stepped across the hull of another old boat, until at last we were walking on the deck of the K-19 itself. Now we were standing where Zateyev himself had stood. This was the deck where his men huddled and shivered during the crisis, exiled there by the captain to keep their radiation exposure down to a minimum. A few feet below us were the compartments that had contained the reactors, the nuclear furnaces in which those young submariners had knowingly given up their lives.

The sight of all these once magnificent boats, with their lethal, streamlined beauty, rusting away in the Arctic Ocean was unsettling to say the least. At the same time, this sad spectacle was not out of keeping with many other things we had seen in Russia, the aftereffects of the Cold War that all but exhausted this enormous nation's already overextended resources, a chronic, systemic depletion that its citizens are still living with on a daily basis.

The Cold War, after all, was not just a military chess game, an effort to maintain the balance of nuclear power, with that wonderful concept Mutual Assured Destruction. It was also a war in a much more literal sense, a war of attrition. Our strategy in constantly upping the ante in the arms race was to push the entire Soviet system to the breaking point. And of course, that strategy succeeded. The Cold War is over, and we were the winners. The walls and the fences have fallen, and we can applaud the fact. But perhaps now we can also allow ourselves to look at the human cost of that war, like victorious soldiers wandering through a bombed-out city and as human beings mourning the fact that this destruction was ever necessary.

Obviously I hope that this movie will be successful and entertaining, a "good ride" as people in Hollywood like to say. It certainly has all the elements, and the performances of Harrison Ford, Liam Neeson, Peter Sarsgaard, and many others brought the unsung heroes of 1961 to life in a way that far exceeded my expectations.

But at times I allow myself to hope that *K-19* will also have another role to play, that it can help to throw open the narrow ideological window through which we, as Americans, have viewed a particular past and culture. In those moments I'm thinking back over the many disquieting things I saw in Russia, and most of all of the people I met there: Our former enemies whose great courage we may now, finally, after all these years, be prepared to acknowledge.

SOVIET/RUSSIAN NAVAL ACCIDENTS

=====

APPENDIX

1952 15 DECEMBER
Project 613 Whiskey-class diesel attack submarine *S-117* sank in the
Pacific Ocean. All 47 crewmen lost.

1955 29 OCTOBER
Battleship *Novorossysk* (previously the Italian ship *Giulio Cesare*) explodes
and sinks in Sevastopol. Six hundred and eight men were lost, and many
were entombed alive. It was the largest single naval peacetime disaster in a century. A monument to the dead stands in Sevastopol.

1956 21 NOVEMBER
Baltic Fleet *M-200*, Quebec-class diesel submarine, the first named
Komsomolets, collided with a destroyer, suffered a fire ignited by liquid
oxygen, exploded, and sank, near Tallinn, Estonia. Twenty-eight
crewmen died, with 7 survivors. A monument to the dead stands
in Paldisky.

1957 22 AUGUST
Black Sea Fleet Project 613, Whiskey-class diesel submarine sinks off
the Crimean coast in 120 feet of water from flooding through a partially closed valve into the diesel engine compartment and a subsequent fire. The entire crew survived entombment for four days. Sub
salvaged 26 August.

1957 26 SEPTEMBER
Baltic Fleet diesel Project 615, Quebec-class, M-256 sank in the Baltic. Thirty-five crewmen were lost.

1959 19 MAY
Baltic Fleet, S-99, prototype combined-diesel-gas turbine, project 617, suffered explosion in gas turbine at 240 feet of water. Succeeded in surfacing, returned to base, and was scrapped. Casualties unknown.

1960 13 OCTOBER
Northern Fleet November SSN K-8 suffers casualty to reactor steam generating tube in the Barents Sea. Thirteen crewmen were seriously irradiated. The submarine returned to base.

1961 27 JANUARY
Northern Fleet modified Project 613, Whiskey-class, twin-cylinder diesel S-80, sank in the Barents Sea in 200 meters of water. Sixty-eight men were lost. The submarine was configured as the first cruise missile-equipped diesel. After testing the missile canisters, a missile tube leak caused the sinking. The sub was salvaged in July 1969. A monument to the lost stands in Polyarny.

1961 4 JULY
Northern Fleet Hotel-class, K-19, suffered a reactor accident, with eight dead and many others exposed to severe radiation. Thirteen crewmen died later. Prototype SSBN suffered a reactor primary cooling system leak en route to the Northern Fleet test range. The reactor was replaced. Submarine resumed operations in 1962. A small monument in Moscow's Kuzminski cemetery honors five of the dead. In Leningrad's Krasnensky cemetery, two of the lost are honored. A single casualty from K-19 is honored in Zelenograd outside Leningrad.

1962 11 JANUARY
Northern Fleet Project 641, Tango-class, B-37, diesel submarine. A torpedo exploded while the submarine was at homeport, and it sank. One hundred and thirty-two people died; 59 B-37 crewmen and 19 aboard adjacent submarines. A monument to the dead stands in Polyarny.

1965
Northern Fleet November-class, *K-11*. Suffered a reactor accident in Severodvinsk. Seven men in the repair party were seriously irradiated when the reactor suffered an uncontrolled power surge while charging the plant.

1965 FEBRUARY
The icebreaker *Lenin* suffered the first nuclear accident. Operator error starved the reactor core of cooling water, damaging the reactor fuel. Thirty crewmen were fatally irradiated. Sixty percent of the fuel assemblies were damaged. The remaining 124 fuel assemblies, the neutron absorbing rods, and quench baffles were removed and dumped in Tsivoli Bay of Novaya Zemlya. The ship was towed to Novaya Zemlya and decontaminated. A second accident occured in 1967 when the primary loop coolant line ruptured and breached containment. The ship was towed to Novaya Zemlya, where the damaged 3,500-ton reactor was encased in concrete, cutout, then blasted with dynamite through the hull into the sea. The icebreaker was towed to Severodvinsk and left until May 1970 when a new reactor was installed. The ship was taken out of service and is now moored with reactors still aboard one kilometer from the center of the city of Murmansk. Plans are underway to convert the icebreaker into a museum at a cost of one million dollars.

1967 15 JULY
Northern Fleet Project 641, Tango-class, diesel submarine *B-31*, suffered a fire in the central command post while in the Mediterranean. Four crewmen were killed.

1967 8 SEPTEMBER
Northern Fleet Project 627, November-class, *K-3*, *Leninsky Komsomol* (the first Soviet nuclear submarine built) lost 39 crewmen in a fire in the first and second compartments while in the Norwegian Sea, 1770 miles from their homeport while returning from under the polar ice. A monument to the dead stands in Zapadnaya Litsa.

1968 8 MARCH
Pacific Fleet Project 629, Golf II-class, SSB, *K-129* sank in the Pacific Ocean with all hands, 98 men, lost. The U.S.S. *Halibut* later found the wreck, and the forward part of the hull was raised with the *Glomar*

Explorer. The Soviets claimed that a collision with an American ship caused the sinking. A monument to the dead stands in Rybachi, Petropavlovsk-Kamchatka.

1968 10 APRIL
Northern Fleet Project 675, Echo II-class, *K-172* on patrol in the Mediterranean, suffered contamination of one compartment with mercury vapor. The entire crew was poisoned, and the number of fatalities are unknown.

1968 24 MAY
Northern Fleet Project 645, November-class *K-27*, with prototype liquid-metal cooled reactor (lead-bismuth) suffered a nuclear accident off Severomorsk. Reactor fuel elements reached 1,000 degrees Celsius; radioactive levels reached 2,000 roentgens per hour in the reactor compartment and in portions of the Central Command Post. Of the 142 crewmen exposed to radiation, six died immediately, four died later, and 12 were gravely radiated. The hull was abandoned until scuttled with reactors in Stepov Bay in Kara Sea, 6 September 1981, at a depth of 60 feet.

1968 23 AUGUST
Northern Fleet Yankee II-class SSBN, *K-140*, suffered an uncontrolled reactor power surge in port. There were no casualties. One damaged reactor was later dumped in the Kara Sea.

1968 10 OCTOBER
Northern Fleet Yankee I-class, *K-26*, suffered a fire, one crewman died of asphyxiation.

1969 15 NOVEMBER
Northern Fleet Project 658M, Hotel-class, SSBN, *K-19* collided with the U.S.S. *Gato* (SSN-615) at 180 feet in the Barents Sea. There were no personnel casualties, and the submarine returned to base.

1970 10 JANUARY
Project 641, Foxtrot-class, diesel attack submarine collided with the Italian *Angelina Laura* in the Bay of Naples. The submarine lost half of her bow and four nuclear torpedoes. There were no personnel casualties.

1970 8 April
Northern Fleet Project 627, November-class SSN, *K-8* sinks off the coast of Spain after a fire in the third and seventh compartments. The submarine was initially abandoned until Moscow ordered it re-manned in a salvage attempt. All 52 crewmen who reboarded the hull were lost when the sub sank suddenly in 14,000 feet. A monument to the lost stands in Severomorsk.

1970 20 June
Pacific Fleet Echo II SSGN, *K-877* believed lost in collision with U.S.S. *Tautog* (SSN-639). Soviet Admiral Aleksin claims in 1993 that the submarine returned safely to base.

1970 late
Alpha-class submarine suffered a reactor meltdown. It was cut into pieces and dumped into the Kara Sea. Casualties are unknown.

1972 24 February
A second reactor accident occurred aboard the Northern Fleet Hotel II-class SSBN, *K-19*. Twenty-eight crewmen died in a fire in compartments eight and nine while on patrol in the Atlantic, 600 miles NE of Newfoundland. Twelve crewmen were trapped for 24 days in the submarine's tenth compartment during a storm. The submarine returned to Severomorsk on April 4.

1973 14 June
Pacific Fleet Project 675, Echo II-class SSGN, *K-56*, collided with the research ship *Akademic Berg*. Twenty-seven submariners and one shipyard specialist died.

1973 31 August
Northern Fleet Yankee I-class SSBN, *K-219* suffered a fuel leak in missile Silo 15. One sailor was killed while trying to put out a fire in the empty silo. The submarine returned to homeport with damage.

1973 5 September
Northern Fleet Echo II-class nuclear submarine was hit by artillery from Soviet surface ship in exercises off Cuba. Casualties were unknown.

1974 31 August
Kashin-class missile destroyer, *Otvazhny* exploded and burned in the Black Sea 120 miles southwest of Sevastopol. Twenty-four crewmen died.

1975 7 November
Baltic fleet Krivak-class frigate *Storozhevoy's* crew mutinied in the Baltic, with an unknown number of casualties. Political officer, Captain 2nd Rank Valeri Sablin was executed following a chase into Swedish waters.

1976 28 August
Echo II-class SSGN collided with U.S.S. *Voge* (DE 1047) in the Mediterranean. No personnel casualties.

1977 8 September
Pacific Fleet Delta I-class SSBN, *K-171* jettisoned a missile with a nuclear warhead, near Kamchatka, following a leak and build-up of pressure in the launch silo. The warhead was later recovered.

1977 10 September
Pacific fleet Yankee I-class, *K-403* suffered a battery explosion with many of the crew injured.

1978 28 December
Pacific fleet Project 667, Delta I-class SSBN, *K-171* reactor suffered a failure of two steam generator tubes. Three crewmen died; neglect by crew was officially cited. The reactors were dumped in 3,000 meters.

1980 21 August
Pacific Fleet Project 659, Echo I-class SSN, suffered a fire 85 miles off the eastern coast of Okinawa. Nine crewmen died, and 50 were evacuated in the Sea of Japan wearing white cloaks. The submarine was towed to Vladivostok.

1980 30 November
Northern Fleet prototype Project 661, Papa-class *K-162*, nuclear-powered submarine suffered an uncontrolled reactor power surge in the Severodvinsk shipyard, resulting in the destruction of the reactor primary loop. Casualties unknown.

1981 21 OCTOBER

Pacific Fleet Project 613, Whiskey-class diesel attack submarine, *S-178* suffered an explosion and fire following a collision with Soviet Refrigerator Ship *Number 13*. The submarine sank in 96 feet near Vladivostok, with 32 men lost. The dead are buried in the Maritime Cemetery in Vladivostok.

1981 27 OCTOBER

Baltic Fleet Project 613, Whiskey-class diesel attack submarine, *S-137* ran aground in Swedish waters off Karlskrona. The commanding officer was later court-martialed.

1983 JUNE

Pacific Fleet Victor III-class SSGN, *K-324* from the Pacific Base of Rakushka collided with the Chinese Han-class SSN near Putyatin Island, 100 km southeast of Vladivostok in Sea Area 99. The Han left parts of screws and rudder imbedded in the Victor III's bow. The commanding officer of *K-324*, Captain Second Rank Viktor Ushakov, claimed that the Han sank to a depth of one km near Ashkold Island, with the loss of its entire 70-man crew. A Soviet survey in 1989 by the Far East Branch of Academy of Sciences, commissioned by Pacific Fleet, detected extremely high radiation levels measuring 1,000 roentgen per hour within a five-mile radius of the broken hull of the Han SSN. Obituaries appearing in Chinese newspapers confirmed that many Chinese senior submarine designers were lost in a submarine accident in 1983.

1983 23 JUNE

Pacific Fleet Project 670, Charlie I-class SSGN, *K-429* sank during a damage-control drill when seawater flooded through an open missile tube. Sixteen crewmen were lost in the Bay of Krachennikov, 4.5 miles from shore. The boat was salvaged in 1983.

1984 13 MAY

An explosion in Severomorsk destroyed the entire Northern Fleet missile storage complex, with more than 200 lives lost.

1984 18 JUNE

Northern Fleet Project 675, Echo II-class SSGN, *K-131* suffered a fire while in the Barents Sea. Thirteen men were lost and buried in Vidayevo. The submarine was later salvaged.

1984 18 September
Pacific Fleet Project 629, Golf II-class SSB, snared a Japanese fishing net cable, which caused a fire from an electrical overload and pulled the trawler *Sumiyoshi Maru* backward before the cable could be cut. Thirteen crewmen died. The submarine returned to homeport under its own power.

1984 21 September
Northern Fleet Project 671,Victor I-class SSN, hit an escort Soviet tanker under the hull while practicing covert transit in the Strait of Gibraltar, ripping off the bow, exposing torpedo tubes and sonar. Casualties unknown.

1985 10 August
Pacific Fleet Project 675, Echo II-class SSGN, *K-431*, while refueling in Chazhma Bay, the fuel rod assembly was accidentally lifted. In the ensuing explosion and fire, ten men were vaporized and the reactor cover blown off. The reactors were removed and the submarine beached to prevent sinking, with heavy contamination to the surrounding area. The submarine was decommissioned and now is moored at the same port with her reactor compartment removed and stored.

1986 3 October
Northern fleet Yankee I-class *K-219* missile exploded. The resulting fire killed four. The ship sank off the coast of Bermuda with 36 nuclear missile warheads and eight nuclear-tipped torpedoes. A dramatic emergency manual reactor shut-down by Seaman Engineer Sergei Preminin prevented nuclear catastrophe. A monument to the young sailor stands in Murmansk.

1986 20 October
The Soviet Navy claimed that the U.S.S. *Augusta* (SSN-710) collided with Delta-1 SSBN *K-279* in the eastern Atlantic. Commanding Officer Boris Apanasenko and Executive Officer Vladimir Tarasenko later stated that they surfaced to check the damage, and the *Augusta* remained submerged, returning to Groton shipyard in New London on October 27 for repairs, estimated at 3 million dollars of damage to her bow.

1988 1 NOVEMBER
Nuclear icebreaker *Rossiya* suffered a near meltdown in Murmansk when secondary coolant of one reactor was accidentally released.

1989 7 APRIL
Northern Fleet Project 685, Mike-class nuclear attack submarine, *K-278, Komsomolets* sank in the Norwegian Sea after a fire. Forty-two crewmen died. A monument to the dead stands in Murmansk.

1991 26 JANUARY
Pacific Fleet Project 641, Foxtrot-class diesel attack submarine, sank while docked at Vladivostok. There were no casualties, and the submarine was raised.

1992 11 FEBRUARY
Northern Fleet Sierra-class SSN collided with U.S.S. *Baton Rouge* off the Kola Peninsula.

1992 15 MAY
Black Sea Fleet Project 877, Kilo-class diesel attack submarine, *B-596*, experienced a rebellion aboard. The conflict resulted in a preliminary agreement to split the Black Sea Fleet between the Russian Federation and the Ukraine.

1993 20 MARCH
Northern Fleet Project 667, Delta IV-class SSBN, and U.S.S. *Greyling* collided in the Barents Sea. There were no casualties. The Commanding Officer of the Russian sub, Captain First Rank Andrei Bulgarkov provided the author a photo of the collision damage.

1994 18 MAY
Pacific Fleet ammunition storage dump explodes. Casualties are unknown.

2000 12 AUGUST
Northern Fleet Project 949, Oscar II-class SSGN, *K-141 Kursk* exploded and sank in 356 feet of water north of the Kola Gulf. One hundred and eighteen crewmen were lost. The submarine was salvaged in October 2001.

Primary Sources

BIBLIOGRAPHY

Interviews, Memoranda of Conversation
* Indicates Russian language source

Andreev, Gennady Alekseyevich, Captain First Rank, Former Commanding Officer Yankee-class SSBN, Flag Missile Specialist, Ghadzhievo Division. Interview, St. Petersburg, 2 October 1995.

Antonov, Gennady Nikolaevich, Rear Admiral, Former Commanding Officer Delta-class SSBN, Chief Naval Missile Directorate, On Sight Inspection Directorate, Russian Defense Ministry. Interview, St. Petersburg, 2 October 1995.

Argunov, Sergei, Captain First Rank, Former Commanding Officer, Charlie II-class SSGN, Pacific Fleet which trailed U.S.S. *Enterprise* CVN 65 during her May 1978 transit to the Western Pacific. Interview, St. Petersburg, 27 September 1995.

Britanov, Igor A., Captain 1st Rank, former Commanding Officer and survivor of Yankee-class SSBN *K-219*. Interview, Moscow, 8 November 1994.

Bystrov, Rear Admiral, First Deputy Chief of Main Navy Staff for Operations and Plans, U.S.S.R. Memorandum of Conversation, Washington, D.C., 8-14 July 1989.

Chernavin, Lev Davidovich, Rear Admiral, Former Foxtrot SS CO and Division Commander during 1962 Cuban Crisis, Chief of cruiser *Aurora* History Directorate. Interview, St. Petersburg, 29 September 1995.

Chernavin, Vladimir. N., Admiral of the Fleet, Commander in Chief Soviet Navy, Memcon. Moscow, 6 October 1989, 14 July 1992, St. Petersburg, 29 July 1996.

Chifonov, Rear Admiral, Deputy Chief of Board of Investigation of the sinking of Yankee-class SSBN *K-219*, Commanding Officer Delta IV-class SSBN. Interview, Moscow, 8 November 1994.

Dygalo, Viktor Ananevich, Rear Admiral, Commander, Division in which Golf II SSB *K-129* assigned, (sank in Pacific 8 March 1968, raised by U.S. CIA Op. *Jennifer*). Former Editor *Morskoi Sbornik*. Interview, Moscow, 23 September 1996.

Gerashenko, Vasili Vladimirovich, Warrant Officer, Survivor of Mike-class *Komsomolets* sinking, 7 April 1989. Interview, St. Petersburg, 28 September 1995.

Ivanov, Vladimir Petrovich, Rear Admiral, Former Director Soviet Naval Counter-Intelligence 1986-1991. Interview, St. Petersburg, 1 October 1996.

Kalistratov, Nikolai, Yakoblevich, General Director Scientific Production Directorate, Little Star, (Nuclear Submarine Construction and Training Yard) Severodvinsk, Russia. Interview, St. Petersburg, 30 July 1996.

Kapitanets, Admiral, First Deputy CinC Soviet Fleet and former Northern Fleet Commander. Memcon. Moscow, July 10, 1989.

Kapitulsky, Gennady, Ya., Captain 3rd Rank, Former main propulsion engineer, survivor of Yankee-class SSBN *K-219*. Interview, St. Petersburg, 15 November 1994, 26 September 1995.

Khvatov, Admiral, CinC Pacific Fleet. Memcon. Vladivostok, 12 July 1990.

Khronopulo, Admiral, CinC Black Sea Fleet. Memcon. Sevastopol, 9 August 1988; 4-8 August 1989; 10 Oct 1989.

Kipyatkova, Anna I., Director Underwater Shipbuilding History, Central Design Bureau for Marine Engineering, *Rubin*. Interview, St. Petersburg, 26 September 1995.

Kochergin, Igor, N., Captain 3rd Rank, Former medical officer, and survivor of Yankee-class SSBN *K-219*. Interviews, St. Petersburg, 15 November 1994 and 1 August 1996.

Komarov, B. M., Vice Admiral, First Deputy Chief of Main Naval Staff for Operations and Plans. Memcon. Moscow, Sevastopol, 4-9 June 1988, 6 August 1989.

Kormilitsin, Chief Constructor, Central Design Bureau for Mike-class SSN *Komsomolets*, Marine Engineering, *Rubin*. Interview, St. Petersburg, 25 September 1995.

Krasnov, Engels Yakovlyevich, Rear Admiral, Chief Broad Ocean Area Ballistic Missile Tests 1970-1975, Frunze classmate and close friend of Nikolai Fedorovich Artamonov. Interview with Lev Vtorygin, St. Petersburg, 1 September 1996.

Krause, Vladimir, Alexeevich, Captain First Rank, GRU, Former Assistant Soviet Naval Attache Ottawa and Washington D.C., 1986-1990. Interviews, 8-13 November 1994.

Kurdin, Igor, K., Captain 1st Rank, Former Exec Officer, Yankee-class *K-219,* and Commanding Officer Delta IV-class, *K-459.* Interviews, St. Petersburg, 15 November 1994, 18 September–2 October 1995.

Kuzmin, Vice Admiral, First Deputy CinC Rear Services, Northern Fleet. Memcon. Severomorsk, Moscow, Sevastopol, 8-13 October, 1989.

Loikanen, Gary Genrikovich, Rear Admiral, Former Commander of a Northern Fleet Yankee Flotilla. Interview, St. Petersburg, 27 September 1995.

Makhonin, Admiral, Former First Deputy Chief of Soviet Main Navy Staff for Logistics 1988-1991. Interview, Moscow, 14 November 1994.

Moiseev, General of the Army, Former Chief of Soviet General Staff 1988-1991. Interview, Moscow, 14 November 1994.

Muru, N. P., Captain First Rank, Dr. of Engineering, Professor, Survivor of the battleship *Novorossysk* rescue and salvage in 1955. Interviews, St. Petersburg, 15 November 1994 and 27 September 1995.

Musatenko, Roman Ivanovich, Captain First Rank, former Yankeee SSBN CO, Director Weapons Faculty, War College. Interview, St. Petersburg, 28 September 1995.

Mushketov, Mikhail P., Captain Second Rank, Assistant Director, Central Naval Museum. Interview, 26 September 1995.

Navoytsev, Pitr Nikolaevich, Admiral, Former First Deputy of Maine Navy Staff for Operations, 1975-1987. Interview in Washington, D.C., 18-24 June 1987 while escorting Soviet delegation U.S./U.S.S.R. Annual Incidents at Sea Talks.

Nikitin, Yu., Captain 2nd Rank, Author. Interview, Moscow, 8 November 1994.

Ovcharenko, Alexsei Mikhailovich, Rear Admiral, Former diesel submarine commander and flotilla commander. Interview, St. Petersburg, 27 September 1995.

Petrachkov, Alexei, Cadet at Nakhimov Naval Preparatory School, Son of Captain 3rd Rank Petrachkov, Former weapons officer, killed during incident aboard SSBN Yankee *K-219*. Interview, St. Petersburg, 15 November 1994.

Ponikarovskiy, Valentin Nikolaevich, Admiral, Former CO November-class SSN, Deputy Northern Fleet Commander for Submarine Operations, Superintendent, St. Petersburg Naval War College. Interview, St. Petersburg, 29 September 1995.

Romanov, Dimitri Andreevich, Former Chief Design Constructor, Central Design Bureau for Marine Engineering. *Rubin*, Deputy Chairman Memorial Foundation for Remembering Submarine *Komsomolets*. Interview, St. Petersburg, 27 September 1995.

Rusin, Alexandr, Engineer Captain First Rank, Staff Black Sea Fleet. Interviews, Sevastopol, 4-10 August 1989.

Rusin, Vyechaslav, Lieutenant Medical Corps, Medical Officer aboard cruiser *Kirov*. Interview, Severomorsk, 13 October 1989.

Russin, Yuri Sergeevich, Rear Admiral, Former Chief of Staff Kamchatka Flotilla, to which Golf II-class SSB *K-129*, was assigned. Interview.

Rutskoi, Alexander, V., Vice President, Russian Federation, Memcon. Moscow, 5 September, 1991.

Selivanov, Ye. V., Chief of Staff, Black Sea Fleet, 1985-1989, Commander, Leningrad Naval Base, 1989-1992. Memcon. Sevastopol, 4-8 August 1989; Leningrad, 28 July 1990. Chief of Main Navy Staff, Interview, Moscow, 20 September 1995.

Shevardnadze, Eduard, Former Foreign Minister, U.S.S.R. Memcon. Moscow, 20 June 1991; Interview, 5 September 1991.

Vtorygin, Lev Alekseevich, Captain First Rank, GRU, Former Soviet Naval Attaché Washington, D.C., 1960-1964. Interview, Moscow, 13 November 1994, 23 September 1995, 30 July 1996; Raymond, Maine, 29 September through 6 October 1996.

Yazov, Dmitry, Marshal, Minister of Defense, U.S.S.R., Memcon. Sevastopol, 9 August, 1988.

Zadorin, Captain 1st Rank, Former Executive Assistant to the CinC Soviet Fleet V. N. Chernavin, 1985-1991. Interview, Moscow, 8 November 1994.

PRIVATE AND GOVERNMENT DOCUMENTS AND STUDIES

Bellona Report Volume Two, "The Russian Northern Fleet–Potential Risk of Radioactive Contamination of the Region," Thomas Nilsen, Igor Kudrik, Alexander Nikitin. Moscow: Bellona Foundation, 19 April 1996.

Bellona Report Volume Three, "The Arctic Nuclear Challenge," Nils Bomer, Aleksandr Nikitin, Igor Kudrik, Thomas Nilsen, Michael McGovern, Andrey Zolotov. Moscow: Bellona Foundation, 13 June 2000.

Decommissioning of Nuclear Facilities: "Decommissioning of Nuclear Powered Submarines," Conference Documentation, Dr. John H. Large, Large and Associates Ltd., Conference Organized by IBC Technical Services, Ltd., 10-11 February 1993.

Deep Sea Radiological Environmental Monitoring Conducted at the Site of the Nuclear-Powered Submarine U.S.S. *Thresher* Sinking. (R/V LULU Voyage 119 and ORV Cape Florida Cruise CF-83-11A, August 2-12, 1983; and R/V ATLANTIS II Voyage #117 Leg #1, August 19-September 15, 1986). Richard B. Sheldon and John D. Michne. October 1993. KAPL, Inc. Knolls Atomic Power Laboratory, Schenectady, New York. KAPL-4748.

Deep Sea Radiological Environmental Monitoring Conducted at the Site of the Nuclear-Powered Submarine U.S.S. *Scorpion* Sinking. (R/V ATLANTIS II Voyage #117 Leg #1, August 19–September 15, 1986) Richard B. Sheldon and John D. Michne. October 1993. KAPL, Inc. Knolls Atomic Power Laboratory, Schenectady, New York. KAPL-4749.

Greenpeace Trip Report: Subject: "Radioactive Waste Situation in the Russian Pacific Fleet, Nuclear Waste Disposal Problems, Submarine Decommissioning, Submarine Safety, and Security of Naval Fuel." Joshua Handler, Research Coordinator, Disarmament Campaign, 27 October 1994.

Greenpeace Working Paper, "Soviet Submarine Accidents and Submarine Safety." Joshua Handler, Research Coordinator, Greenpeace Nuclear Free Seas Campaign, Washington, D.C., 4 September 1991.

Greenpeace, "Spying Beneath the Waves: Nuclear Submarine Intelligence Operations–An extract from "The Nuclear Navy." Prepared by Hans M. Kristensen, Greenpeace International, August 1994.

Greenpeace, "Soviet/Russian Submarine Accidents:1956-1994." Joshua Handler, Research Coordinator, Greenpeace International Disarmament Campaign, 9 October 1994.

Greenpeace, "Testimony for the U.S. Senate Permanent Subcommittee on Threat Posed by the Proliferation of Weapon of Mass Destruction," by Joshua Handler, Greenpeace Disarmament Campaign, 13 March 1996.

Neptune Papers No. Three, "Naval Accidents 1945-1988." William M. Arkin and Joshua Handler, Greenpeace, Institute for Policy Studies, June 1989.

Russian Nuclear-Powered Submarine Decommissioning, Oleg Bukharin and Joshua Handler. Amsterdam, Science and Global Security, 1995, Volume 5, pp. 245-271.

Tragedy and Triumph: The Sinking and Salvage of Battleship Novorossysk, Murmu, N. P., Doctor of Technical Science, professor, engineer, survivor of the search and rescue in 1955. Unpublished personal manuscript, 1993.*

U.S. Council for Energy Awareness, Study Source Book, 1992. Soviet-Designed Nuclear Power Plants in the Former Soviet Republics and Czechoslovakia, Hungary and Bulgaria. U.S. Council for Energy Awareness, 1776 I Street, NW, Washington, D.C., 20006-3708.

"Yablokov Report," Facts and Problems Related to Radioactive Waste Disposal in Seas Adjacent to the Territory of the Russian Federation *(Materials for a Report by the Government Commission on Matters Related to Radioactive Waste Disposal at Sea,* Created by Decree No. 613 of the Russian Federation President, October 24, 1992). Office of the President of the Russian Federation, Moscow 1993.

AUTOBIOGRAPHIES, MEMOIRS, AND FIRSTHAND ACCOUNTS

Agar, Augustin, *VC, Baltic Episode: A Classic of Secret Service in Russian Waters.* London: Conway Maritime Press, 1963.

Burov, Vladimir Nikolaevich, Vice Admiral, *Otechestvennoe Voennoe Korablestroenie V Tretyem Stoleti Svoeii Istorii (Patriotic Naval Shipbuilding During the Past 300 Years).* St. Petersburg: Federal Program of Russian Publishers, 1995.*

Chernavin, Vladimir N., Admiral of the Fleet, *The Log*: "The Fleet and The Destiny of Russia." Moscow: Andreevski Flag, 1993.*

_____ , *Atomi Podvodni'* (Atoms Underwater). Moscow: Andreevski Flag, 1993.*

Colby, William and Peter Forbath, *Honorable Men.* New York: Simon and Schuster, 1978.

Courtney, Anthony, Commander, *Sailor in a Russian Frame.* London: Johnson, 1968.

Custine, Marquis, *Journey of Our Time.* New York: Pelligrini and Cudahy, 1956.

Daniloff, Nicholas, *Two Lives, One Russia.* New York: Avon, 1988.

Djilas, Milovan, *Conversations With Stalin.* New York: Harcourt Brace and World, 1962.

Gorbachev, Mikhail S., *Memoirs.* New York: Doubleday, 1995.

Kalugin, Oleg with Fen Montaigne, *The First Directorate: My Thirty-Two Years in Intelligence and Espionage Against the West.* New York: St. Martin's Press, 1994.

Mikhailovski, Arkadi, P., Admiral, *Vertikalnoye Vspl'itie (Blow to the Surface).* St. Petersburg: Nauka, 1995.*

Mormul Nikolai, *Atomnye Unikalnye Strategicheskie, Zapiski Ispyitalyelya Atomnikh Podvodnikh Lodok* (Memoirs of Nuclear Submarine Trials). Murmansk: Dom, 1997.*

Romanov, D. A., *Tragediya Pdvodvodnoi Lodki Komsomolets, Argumenti Konstrucktura (Tragedy of Submarine* Komsomolets, *Arguments of the Constructor).* St. Petersburg: Peasant and Humanitarian Institute Press, 1995.*

Samoylov, V., Admiral (Reserve), "Seventeen Hundred Meters Down Aboard the *Komsomolets,*" *Morskoi Sbornik,* Vol. 4, September 1992, p. 33-36.*

Soviet General Staff Archives, "Anadyr." File Six, Volume 2, p. 144, Moscow, 1962.*

Standley, William H. and Arthur A. Ageton, *Admiral Ambassador to Russia.* Chicago: H. Regnery, 1955.

Stevens, Leslie, *Russian Assignment.* Boston: Little Brown, 1955.

Tolley, Kemp, *Caviar and Commissars: The Experiences of a U.S. Naval Officer in Stalin's Russia.* Annapolis: Naval Institute Press, 1983.

Zavarin, V., "In Memory of the Living," *Morskoi Sbornik*, No. 6, 1990, pp. 42-46.*

Zhiltsov, Lev; Nicolai Mormoul; Leonid Ossipenko, *La Dramtique Histoire Des Sous-Marins Nucleaires Sovietiques: Des exploits, des echecs et des catastrophes cachees pendant trente ans.* Paris: Robert Laffont, 1992.

_____ . *Atomnaya Podvodnaya Epopeya: Exploits, Misfortune, Catastrophes.* Moscow: A/O "Borgee," 1994.*

NEWSPAPER ARTICLES

Allyn, Bruce J. and James G. Blight, "Closer Than We Knew." *The New York Times,* November 2, 1992. Letters, p. A18.

Atlas, Terry, "Old Russian Nuclear Subs Pose Environmental Threat, Study Says," *Chicago Tribune*, February 26, 1993. Section 1, p. 5.

Babashin, Gerald, *"Tragediya V Rezhime Molchaniya"* (Tragedy in the Regime of Silence), *Sem'ya*, No.11, St. Petersburg, 1997.

Bivens, Matt, "Soviet Captain Recounts Tale of a 'Chernobyl' Under Sea." *The Nation*, Bankok, Thailand, 21 May 1993, p. 1.

Black, Norman, "Augusta Likely Hit Soviet Sub," *The Day*, New London, Connecticut, 2 March 1987.

Bobkov, B. N., "Why No Foreign Sources on Diversionary Tactics?", *Krasnaya Zvezda*, 21 May 1988.*

Bohlen, Celestine, "Soviet A-Sub Blaze Off Bermuda Kills Three", *The Washington Post*, October 5 1986.

Bushev, Aleksandr, "Kontr-Admiral Mormul' Idiet Na Dno" (Kontr Admiral Mormul Goes Bottoms Up), *Komsomolskaya Pravda,* Moscow, 27 December 1995.*

Broad, William J. "Navy Has Long Had Secret Subs." *The New York Times*, 7 February 1994. pp. A1-B7.

_____, "Disasters With Nuclear Subs In Moscow's Fleet Reported," *The New York Times*. International, 26 February 1993.

_____, "Sunken Sub to Be Tested for Nuclear Leaks," *The New York Times*, 1 August 1993, p. 8.

_____, "Hazard Is Doubted From Sunken Sub," *The New York Times*, 5 September 1993.

_____, "Russians to Seal Sunken Nuclear Torpedoes," *The New York Times*, 19 September 1993, p. 19.

Campbell, Matthew, "Revealed: the Real Red October Story," *Sunday Times*, London, 3 October, 1993, p. 1.

Gellman, Barton, "U.S. and Russian Nuclear Subs Collide," *The Washington Post*, Washington, D.C., 22 March 1993.

Getz, Bill, "Ukraine Won't Finish Russian Flattop," *The Washington Times*, 1 January 1997, p. A3.

Gordon, Michael R., "Russians Asked U.S. Aid to Raise Lost Atom Sub," *The New York Times*, 24 November 1993.

Gundarov, Vladimir, "Violation of Rules of Submarine Operations, Together with an Incident of Concealment; Collision of a Russian Atomic Submarine with an American Nuclear Sub (U.S.S. *Greyling*) in the Eyes of Witnesses." *Krasnaya Zvesda*, No. 69-70, 27 March 1993, p. 1.*

Harnon, William H., "Russian and American Pilots Play Chicken," *The New York Times* Magazine, November 22, 1970, p. 25.

Hague, Frederic, "Russian Treason Case Tests New Freedom," *The New York Times*, *Portland Press Herald*, Portland, 27 November 1996, p. 3.

Hoffman, David, "Russia Accuses Ex-Officer of Spying," *The Washington Post*, Washington, D.C., 12 February 1996.

_____, "Russian Ex-Navy Captain Is Charged With Treason," *The Washington Post*, 3 October 1996, p. A29.

_____, "Russian Turmoil Reaches Nuclear Sanctum," *The Washington Post*, 22 December 1996, pp. A34-36.

Kolton, Ilya, "Surface and Show; Secret Documents About the Condition of Submarines in the Russian Fleet," *Sobesednik*, No.12, June 1992, pp. 1-3.*

Nikitin, Yevgeni, "Without the Secret Caveat: The Secret of Submarine *Yankee*," *Rossiskaya Gazeta*, 2 September 1994. p. 6.*

Mellgren, Doug, "Russia's Nuclear Woes Said World Threat," Associated Press, *Potomac News*, Woodbridge, Virginia, 7 December 1994.

Offley, Ed, "Sub that came in from the Cold: Spy vessel finds new home, but is mission familiar?" *Navy Times*, December 12, 1994, p. 8.

_____, "Russian Warships Pose Threat—To Russians," *Seattle Post-Intelligencer*, February 26, 1993, p. A2.

Pincus, Walter, "Military-to-Military Talks on Cuts Suggested," *The Washington Post*, 18 July, 1988, pp. 1-8.

Pitt, David, E., "Pentagon Fights Wider Ocean-Dumping Ban," *The New York Times*, 26 September 1993, p. 8.

Ploskurovskaya, Y., "Extraordinary American Emissary in Moscow," *Moscow Evening News*, 18 July, 1989, p. 3.*

Razumn'iy, A., "Tired of Submarines in the Deep, I Came Home," *Polyarka*, 23 February 1993.*

Smith, R. Jeffrey, "U.S. Officials Acted Hastily In Nuclear Test Accusation, CIA Hesitates to Call Russian Event a Quake," *The Washington Post*, 20 October 1997, pp. A1-A7.

Solovyev, S., "Once More About the Tragedy *Novorossysk*," *Krasnaya Zvezda*, 27 January 1990.*

Strouse, Charles, "At The Moscow Embassy, U.S. Blindsided by Caution," *The Daily Press*, Newport News, Virginia, 22 January 1988, p. 4. Reprinted from *The New Republic*.

Sullivan, Walter, "Soviet Nuclear Dumps Disclosed," *The New York Times*, 24 November 1992, p. C9.

Tutorskaya, S., *Izvestiya*, 11 May 1991.*

Volkogonov, Dmitri, General, "Looking Back: The Search for Information about the Crew of K-129," *Krasnaya Zvezda*, 11 December 1993, pp. 1-4.*

Williams, Daniel, "Legacy of Soviet Nuclear Tests Haunts Kazakhstan," *The Washington Post*, 7 November 1997, pp. A1-A33.

Yakimets, Vladimir, "Splitting the Atom, the First Half- Century." *Sobesednik*, 1994, pp. 3-7.*

Yemelyanekov, Aleksander, "The Navy: In Tragedies at Sea—Conditions Ashore. Unsinkable, From Notes Under the Caveat 'Secret.'" *Sobesednik*, No.14, April 1992, pp. 4-5.*

York, Geoffrey, "Black Sea Imbroglio Strains Ties, Spat Strands Fleet," *The Washington Times*, 30 November 1996, p. A1.

SECONDARY SOURCES AND PERIODICALS

Ablamonov, P. F., *Admiral: Twice Hero of the Soviet Union, S.G.Gorshkov.* Moscow: Publisher of Political Literature, 1986.*

Aleksin, V., Kontr Admiral, "The Case of Operation Jenifer," *Morskoi Sbornik*, 5 June 1992, p. 79-83.*

_____ , "Incident in the Barents Sea," *Morskoi Sbornik*, 5 June, 1992, pp. 21-22.*

_____ , "The Fleet's Accident Rate," *Morskoi Sbornik*, No. 10, 1992, pp. 37-42.*

_____ , "They Died At Action Stations," *Morskoi Sbornik*, No. 12, 1993, pp. 12-14.*

Andrew, Christopher and Oleg Gordievsky, *KGB: The Inside Story From Lenin to Gorbachev.* New York: Harper Collins, 1990.

Beschloss Michael R. and Strobe Talbott, *At The Highest Levels: The Inside Story of the End of the Cold War.* Boston: Little Brown, 1993.

Berezhnoi, S. S., *Flot SSSR Korabli i Suda Lendlisa, Spravochnik* (The U.S.S.R. Fleet, Ships of Lend Lease, and Reference). St. Petersburg: Velen', 1994.*

Boechin, Igor, "Investigating a Catastrophe: Sarcophagus at Bear Island?" *Technika-Molodezhi,* No. 10, 1994, pp. 30-35.*

Brown, Anthony Cave, *The Last Hero.* New York: Time-Life Books, 1982.

Bukan, S. P., *Investigating Underwater Catastrophes.* Moscow: Guild Master "Rus'", 1992.*

Burleson, Clyde W., *The Jennifer Project.* Englewood Cliffs: Prentice-Hall, 1977.

Burov, V. N., *Patriotic Naval Shipbuilding (Otechestvennoe Voennoe Korablectroenie).* St. Petersburg: Sudostroenie, 1995.*

Capelotti, P.J., *Our Man in the Crimea: Commander Hugo Koehler and the Russian Civil War.* Columbia: University of South Carolina Press, 1991.

Cherkashin, Nikolai, "Requiem for a Battleship," from *The Secret Bond that Binds all Seamen.* Moscow: Voenizdat, 1990.*

_____ , *The Log,* "Hiroshima"; Surface at Noon. Moscow: Andreevsky Flag, 1993.*

_____ , *The Log,* "Last Parade"; Chronicle of an Anti-Brezhnev Rebellion. Moscow: Andreevsy Flag, 1992.*

_____ , *The Log,* "Kak Pogibayut Submarini" (How Subs Die). Moscow: Andreevsky Flag, 1995.*

_____ , "Povsednevnaia Zhizn Russuskikh Podvodnikov." Moscow: Molodaia Guardia, 2001.

Corson, William R. and Susan B. Trento, *Widows: Four American Spies, the wives they left behind, and the KGB's crippling of American intelligence.* New York: Crown Publishers, 1989.

Dotsenko, V. D., *Flot v Voina i Pobeda (The Fleet in War and Victory)* 1941-1945. St. Petersburg: Sudostroenie, 1995.*

Drew, Christopher and Sherry Sontag, *Blind Man's Bluff.* New York: Public Affairs, 1999.

Dybski, Kiril, "The Secret of Volume No. 33," *Chest Imayu,* No. 7, 1994, pp. 16-19.*

Erichkson, William, *Lighting the Dark: Revolution in Eastern Europe.* New York: William Morrow and Co. 1990.

Fleming, Peter, *The Fate of Admiral Kolchak.* London: Rupert Hart Davis, 1963.

Grebera, Rene, "Wie Ging Die *Novorossysk* Verloren?" (How was the *Novorossysk* Lost?) *Marine Rundshau,* No. 6, 1989, pp. 369-373.

Golovko, A., *With the Fleet.* Moscow: Progress, 1979.

Guttridge, Leonard, F., *Munity: A History of Naval Insurrection.* Annapolis: Naval Institute Press, 1992.

Handler, Joshua, "No Sleep In the Deep for Russian Subs." *Bulletin of the Atomic Scientists,* April 1993, pp. 7-9.

_____ , "Submarine Safety—The Soviet/Russian Record," *Jane's Intelligence Review,* July 1992–International, pp. 328-332.

Herbig, Jost, *Im Labyrinth der Gebiemdienste: Der Fall: Jennifer (In the Labyrinth of the Secret Service: Operation Jennifer)*. Frankfurt am Main: Fischer, 1981.

Herrick, Robert Waring, *Soviet Naval Strategy*. Annapolis: U.S. Naval Institute Press, 1968.

_____, *Soviet Naval Theory and Policy, Gorshkov's Inheritance*. Annapolis: U.S. Naval Institute Press, 1988.

Hurt, Henry, *Nick Shadrin, The Spy Who Never Came Back*. New York: McGraw Hill, 1981.

Hraptovich, Albert, "We Riveted Hundreds of Floating Targets," *Rossiskaya Gazeta*, October 19, 1994.

Karzhavin, B.A., *Sinking of the* Otvazhniy: *Documentary History of a Naval Catastrophe*. Moscow: Korvet, 1993.*

_____ , *The Sinking of the Battleship* Novorossysk: *Documents and Facts*. St. Petersburg: Polytechnik, 1992.*

_____ , *The Mystery of the Sinking of the Battleship* Novorossysk. St. Petersburg: Polytechnik, 1991.*

_____ , *"Novorossysk*, Lessons of the Tragedy," *Morskoi Sbornik*, No. 4, 1991.*

_____ , *Secret Archives: The Loss of* Otvazhniy. St. Petersburg: Korvet, 1994.*

Kasatanov, V. A., Admiral; Senatski, Yu. K.; Shigin, V. V., *The Log*, "Kholodnaya Voina Poteplenie ili proriv?" (Cold War: Heating Up or a Break?). Moscow: Andreevski Flag, 1995.*

Korshunov, Yuri, "America Discovers Russia," Stari Peterburg, Vol. 24, p. 33, Summer, 1989.*

Kostomarov, V., "Prosti Novorossysk," *Strazh Baltik,* 24 March, 1992.*

Kraus, George R., "Papa, Alfa, and Soviet Submarine Innovation," U.S. Naval Institute *Proceedings*, February1994, pp. 87-88.

Kravtsov, Anatoli, "Investigating An Underwater Chernobyl?" *Ogonyok*, December 1993, pp.44-45.*

Lehovich, Dimitry V., *White Against Red, The Life of General Anton Denikin*. New York: W. W. Norton, 1993.

Leskov, Sergei, "Nuclear Dumping: Lies and Incompetence," The Bulletin of Atomic Scientists, June 1993, pp. 13-14.

Loubat, J., *Fox's Mission to Russia*. New York: 1873.

Minchenko, S., Captain 1st Rank, "Operation Depth," *Morskoi Sbornik*, July, 1994.*

Mitchell, Donald W., *A History of Russian and Soviet Sea Power*. New York: Macmillan, 1974.

Mitchell, Mairin, *Maritime History of the Russians*. Paris: Victor Hugo, 1952.

Mozgovoi, Aleksander, "Secret Concealed Beneath the Waves," *Echo of the Planet*, No. 6, February 1994, pp. 22-27.*

_____ , "Ram 'Hiroshima,'" *Morskoi Sbornik*, No. 11, 1993, pp. 48-50.

Nikitin, Ye., Captain 1st Rank, "Tragedy in the Sagasso Sea," *Morskoi Sbornik*, October 1991, pp. 45-51.*

_____ , "Fateful Bermuda: The Story of *K-219*." Unpublished Manuscript, Moscow: July 1994.*

Oberg, James E., *Uncovering Soviet Disasters: The Limits of Glasnost*. New York: Random House, 1988.

Oberdorfer, Don, *The Turn, From the Cold War to the New Era*. New York: Touchstone, 1991.

Pavlov, Aleksandr S., *Military Vessels of the Soviet Union and Russia 1945-1995*. 3rd edition, Yakutsk, 1994.

Razdolgin, A. A. and Skorikov, Y. A., *Kronstadt Fortress*, Leningrad: Stroyizdat, 1988.*

Remnick, David, *Lenin's Tomb*. New York: Simon and Schuster, 1993.

Ryan, Cornilius, *The Last Battle*. New York: Simon and Schuster, 1966.

Sanders, James, Mark Sauter, Cort Kirkwood, *Soldiers of Misfortune: The Cold War Betrayal and Sacrifice of American POWs*. New York: Avon, 1992.

Savinkin, A. E., Dominin, I. V., *Voenno-Morskaya Ideya Rossii (Russian Naval Ideas)*. Moscow: Military University, 1997.*

Schachte, William L., "The Black Sea Incident," U.S. Naval Institute *Proceedings*, Vol.114/6/1024, p. 12, June, 1988.

Schoenfeld, Gabriel, "Underwatergate, A Submarine Chernobyl," *The New Republic*, 27 April 1993, pp. 20-21.

Shitarev, Viktor, "Secret of the Pacific Ocean," *Technika-Molodozha*, No. 8, 1992, pp. 40-42.*

Shlomin, V., "Andrevskiy Flag," *Morskoi Vestnik* (Naval Digest), No. 6, 1992.*

Sigar, Norman, "Why Did the *Novorossysk* Sink?," *Revista Marina*, Jan 1990.

Stvolinski, Yu, *Konstruktori Podvodnykh Korablyi (Submarine Builders)*. Leningrad: Lenizdat, 1984.

Vali, Ferenc A., *The Turkish Straits and NATO*. Stanford: Hoover Institution Press, 1972.

van Voors, Bruce, "Murky Waters for the Supersub," *Time,* January 25, 1988, p. 26.

Varner, Roy, *A Matter of Risk*. New York: Random House, 1978.

Vego, Milan, *Soviet Naval Tactics*. Annapolis: U.S. Naval Institute Press, 1992.

Watson, Bruce, *Red Navy and Soviet Naval Operations on the High Seas, 1956-1980*. Princeton: Westview Press, 1982.

Weeks, Charles, J., Jr., *An American Naval Diplomat in Revolutionary Russia: The Life and Times of Vice Admiral Newton A. McCully*. Annapolis: U.S. Naval Institute Press, 1993.

Yermolin, Y., Mozgovoi, A. and Nikitin, Y., *Echoes of the Planet*, Issue no. 40, 1991.*

ACKNOWLEDGMENTS

═══════

THIS STORY OF THE *K-19* could not have been told without the years of persistent research by film director Kathryn Bigelow, screenwriter Chris Kyle, and National Geographic producer Christine Whitaker. Only by overcoming staggering obstruction and gaining access to the personal memoir of the former commanding officer of the submarine *K-19* and to the testimony of some surviving crewmen, could the details of this event be reconstructed. This is the first time that the participants in this harrowing episode present their story in their own words. It is also the first time that a Western author uses the views expressed to him by the former senior leaders of the Soviet Navy to fill in some of the remaining voids in the history of the naval Cold War.

This account of a fatal accident in the early years of Soviet Navy nuclear power reveals that the hazards of uncontrolled atomic power were not fully understood by the reactor designers and builders, or the men who took the ships to sea. The *K-19* proved to be a bad omen of what was to come in the next three decades of the Soviet Navy nuclear experience.

John Paine expertly edited the text, and Timothy Sergay painstakingly translated Captain Zateyev's handwritten memoir. Naval nuclear engineer Lars Hanson was our expert reader and helped make the sometimes complex material more readable to the layman. I am grateful to National Geographic Books Editor-in-Chief Kevin Mulroy, and my agent Alexander Hoyt, for providing me the opportunity to write the larger history of the *K-19* after working in the wings for more than three years as a technical advisor for the film. I am also deeply grateful to senior editor Lisa Lytton for her patience and the close working relationship that we shared.

PETER A. HUCHTHAUSEN
Captain, USN (Ret.)

INDEX

PUBLISHED BY THE
NATIONAL GEOGRAPHIC SOCIETY

John M. Fahey, Jr., *President and Chief Executive Officer*

Gilbert M. Grosvenor, *Chairman of the Board*

Nina D. Hoffman, *Executive Vice President*

PREPARED BY THE BOOK DIVISION

Kevin Mulroy, *Vice President and Editor-in-Chief*

Charles Kogod, *Illustrations Director*

Marianne R. Koszorus, *Design Director*

STAFF FOR THIS BOOK

Lisa Lytton, *Editor*

John Paine, *Text Editor*

Timothy D. Sergay, *Translator*

Melissa Farris, *Designer*

Lars P. Hanson, *Researcher*

Gary Colbert, *Production Director*

Ric Wain, *Production Project Manager*

Janet Dustin, *Illustrations Editor*

MANUFACTURING AND
QUALITY CONTROL

Christopher A. Liedel, *Chief Financial Officer*

Phillip L. Schlosser, *Managing Director*

John T. Dunn, *Technical Director*

Vincent P. Ryan, *Manager*

Clifton M. Brown, *Manager*

Alan Kerr, *Manager*

LIBRARY OF CONGRESS CATALOGING-IN-PUBLICATION DATA
Huchthausen, Peter A. 1939-
   K-19 : the widowmaker : the secret story of the Soviet nuclear submarine / Peter A. Huchthausen.
      p. ; cm.
   Includes bibliographical references and index.
   ISBN 0-7922-6472-X (pbk.)
   1. Nuclear submarines--Accidents--Soviet Union. 2. Nuclear submarines--Accidents--Russia (Federation) 3. Submarine disasters--Soviet Union.
   4. Submarine disasters--Russia (Federation) I. Title.

V857.5 .H83 2002
363.12'365'0947--dc21

2002019721